Rock Climbing

Rock Climbing

STEVE ASHTON

The Crowood Press

First published in 1987 by
The Crowood Press
Ramsbury, Marlborough
Wiltshire SN8 2HE

© Steve Ashton 1987

All rights reserved. No part of this publication may be reproduced or transmitted in any form or by any means, electronic or mechanical, including photocopy, recording, or any information storage and retrieval system without permission in writing from the publishers.

British Library Cataloguing in Publication Data

Ashton, Steve
   Rock climbing.
   1. Rock climbing – Great Britain
   I. Title
   796.5'223'0941   GV199.44.G7
   ISBN 0–946284–63–6

Acknowledgements

I would first like to thank my climbing partners of the last eighteen years with whom I learned to take risks and yet (so far at least) stay alive. Their input to this book – no less valuable for being unwitting – has been considerable.

    Thanks also to Tony Ashton for his work on the manuscript, to the members of the BMC Technical Committee for their advice on rope technique; to Dr Tony Jones and Dr Ieuan Jones for suggestions on the emergency checklists; and to Donald Bennet, Aysel Crocket, Ian Smith and Ken Wilson for their excellent photographs.

Fig 17 by Ian Smith; Fig 53 by Aysel Crocket; Fig 129 by Donald Bennet; Fig 138 by Ken Wilson; all other photographs by the author.

Typeset by Inforum Ltd
Printed in Great Britain

Contents

Preface 7
Introduction 8

CLIMBS AND CLIMBERS
1 Rock 12
2 First Climbs 15
3 Leading 22
4 Boulders and Training 28
5 Hard Rock 35

EQUIPMENT
6 Personal Equipment 42
7 Ropes, Karabiners and Knots 50
8 Protection Equipment 61

TECHNIQUES
9 Rock and Rock Climbing Technique 70
10 Rope Technique 80
11 Emergency Rope Techniques 94
12 Some Special Topics 106

ROCK CLIMBING IN BRITAIN
13 A Brief History 117
14 British Crags and Climbs 123

APPENDIX
Grading Systems 139
Glossary 143
Useful Addresses 151
Bibliography 153
Index 157

Preface

The writer of a textbook on rock climbing assumes a tremendous responsibility. It is not enough that the book describes the rudiments of good technique – although it must certainly do that – if it fails to convey something of the true essence of the sport. Conscious of this duty I have arranged the book in four sections, each reflecting an important facet of the sport.

The first section, based on my own early experiences, introduces rock climbing in general terms. Those of you coming fresh to the sport should find this helpful in establishing a context for the more technical information which follows. Those of you already experienced in climbing will find little in it that is new, but you are welcome to snigger at my bumbling progress through this psychological minefield.

The second and third sections deal with equipment and techniques. These sections are the 'meat' of the book and make extensive use of illustrations to help clarify the technicalities. I have tried to concentrate on the fundamental aspects of rock and rope technique, believing that too much too soon would merely confuse the issue.

The fourth section describes the development of rock climbing since its beginnings more than a century ago. The sport's traditions place heavy demands on each new generation, but in return the history which spawned them enriches our appreciation of the cliffs and climbs.

The main text ends with a gazetteer of major climbing grounds. There are many cliffs among them which I have yet to visit, and not until I have grown too feeble to move will I stop wanting to climb them – and maybe not even then. If this book in some way helps you to formulate and realise your own climbing ambitions I shall have paid back some of the great debt I owe to this wonderful sport.

Introduction

Friday evening. Throughout Britain climbers are packing rucksacks and making rendezvous. Soon they will begin to travel towards the hills and coastlines. It doesn't matter how: by coach, minibus, train, motorcycle, battered van or family saloon. Tonight they will erect tents by torchlight, unlock the doors of club huts, unroll sleeping bags in disused cowsheds, or book into hotels. Some will be teenagers; most will be in their early twenties; many will be approaching middle age; while a few will be closer to sixty or seventy. Men and women: students, engineers, factory workers, secretaries, teachers, shop assistants, doctors. Nothing identifies them as rock climbers but their common purpose this Friday night.

Later the talk will be of success and failure on the crags the previous weekend, or of ambitions for the coming season. A tale of outrageous behaviour will receive its hundredth telling, becoming a little more colourful and a lot less truthful on its way into myth and legend. Eventually plans for tomorrow will be developed, each a little too ambitious but fuelled into the realms of possibility by the atmosphere of daring which prevails.

Saturday brings rain, hangovers and paralysing doubts. The morning light floods the valleys only to be sucked into the shadows of the cliffs. Already the cloud begins to curl down from the summits, brushing the rocks with a slippery coat of moisture. The warm glow of anticipation evaporates to leave only the cold gnawing of trepidation.

Rucksacks are heavy, the approach tedious. Muffled shouts fall to earth and betray the presence of others already at work high on the cliff. For a few seconds the mists part to reveal a bizarre mannequin swathed in coloured loops and shining metal, jigging uncertainly from foot to foot and moaning softly. His partner, meanwhile, linked by the rope, hides his pale face inside a cave to fend off vertigo. From time to time they call to each other, as if to relieve the overwhelming sense of loneliness which grips them. The echoes mingle half-way until taken by the wind. The mists close again and they are gone.

Down below things are going no better; some equipment has been forgotten, the rope lies in a tangle. Muttered recriminations threaten to divide the partnership before the climb has properly begun.

The mood changes with the first movements, as if the touch and texture of rock trigger a well-practised routine which has the power to stem the rising tide of uncertainty. This is it. Your body responds by leaning, pulling and pushing in harmony. The process has become an elevated dance, the cliff its tilted stage. Curtains of rock hang to each side as you creep skyward, the rope trailing behind as an anchor on life and reality.

Rhythm and movement falter where the rock begins to bulge out above your head. The fingers of your left hand mechanically curl over a small flake of rock, while your body hangs vertically beneath like a sack suspended from a hook. Meanwhile, the fingers of your right hand begin burrowing into a crack. The knuckles, red with abrasion, bleed gently from a raised flap of skin; but there is no pain and the injury seems unimportant. To ease the strain your legs spread themselves wide, bridging across the opposing walls of the corner. The right leg vibrates with fatigue and threatens to dislodge your foot from its hold. Strength is fading; the next five seconds will be crucial.

The fingers finally lock into the crack. Relief surges through your body. The left arm screams for release, but instead you wrench up on it, kicking free from the puzzle that has pinned you to that one place for so long. A hidden strength peels back the blanket of anxiety; your limbs pull and press together, choreographed by a brain turned hyperactive through adrenalin. The dance resumes, fuelled by gasps of upwelling air.

Exhilaration subsides at the top of the climb while you concentrate on belaying the rope to safeguard your partner's ascent. Soon a feeling of weariness will smother the lingering glow of satisfaction. In silence you will coil the ropes and begin the easy scramble to regain the foot of the cliff, but by then your thoughts will be turning to the next climb and the new problems it will bring. Rock climbing is an addictive drug, and once is not enough.

First movements on rock are often scrambling ones, encountered perhaps while following one of the famous ridge walks. This common ground blurs any theoretical line of demarcation drawn between walking and climbing, so that only when pursued at their extremes do the two experiences appear unrelated.

Having been inspired by early scrambling experiences to take up 'proper' rock climbing, it would be a mistake to delve immediately into the technicalities of ropework. Ropes can interfere badly with the exhilaration of moving unaided and unfettered over steep rock. It is much better to find some local outcrop or quarry and simply climb around its base. The absence of danger will help you shed a debilitating tenseness which often afflicts those first hesitant movements. If one section proves too difficult, simply jump off and start somewhere else – you won't be letting anyone down and you won't feel under pressure to perform.

Bouldering, as this entertaining branch of climbing is known, can be a rewarding pursuit in itself, but there is more to rock climbing than problem solving and athletic movement. What would it be like, you wonder, to be threading a route up one of the really big crags? Here the sort of problems encountered on small outcrops are piled one above the other in a vertical maze – some obvious and challenging, others concealed and lurking – while the proximity of danger adds spice to the adventure.

Such is the nature of the sport that even a mildly ambitious climber will sometimes attempt routes that are a fraction too difficult. On such occasions the risk of falling – always present to some degree – multiplies alarmingly. To combat this, elaborate protection methods are employed. Not that rock climbing can ever be thought completely safe – it never is. In fact, sophistication of rope technique is deliberately suppressed in order to confine equipment to its passive role as a safety net. This preserves the essential

Introduction

nature of the sport so that no amount of ropes and hardware will get you up a difficult climb if your body or spirit is lacking.

You will soon discover that the cliff you aspire to climb – you might have passed below it during a hill walk or seen a photograph in a book on mountains – has been climbed before. In fact, a dozen or more routes will probably have been pioneered up its various facets, the most interesting of them being repeated four or five times every fine weekend. These routes will have names, and their lefts and rights will be meticulously described in a guidebook which you can buy from the local equipment shop. Inevitably, some of the mystery evaporates with this discovery. In compensation the guidebook will reveal a hundred-year-old history of rock climbing which surrounds the cliffs and climbs with intrigue and renown.

Guidebooks, history, and conversations with other climbers, all help to parcel routes into identifiable objectives. This is the 'sport' of rock climbing. It puts names to aspirations and legitimises an activity which otherwise might appear futile. However, there is really no need for justification. Climbers continue to climb because to do otherwise would be unthinkable.

CLIMBS AND CLIMBERS

Fig 1   Nearing the top of Shrike, an exposed E1 on Clogwyn du'r Arddu.

1 Rock

Few sports insist on such intimate contact with the medium as does rock climbing. Skis intervene between skier and snow, the canoe between canoeist and water. In rock climbing that searching and gripping with bare fingers is unique. Despite modern terminology, this is manifestly a primitive action; something a wild animal might do, with its animal fears, strengths and daring.

Your first encounter with rock may ultimately prove to be the most significant. It has the power to shape your whole attitude towards the sport. I know that mine did. I was fifteen years old and struggling miserably with the knots of adolescence. School was a particular problem. Early academic promise had failed to materialise, while my athletic prowess – never astounding at the best of times (a cheerless fourteenth in the annual cross-country) – was fast crumbling in the face of youthful indolence and assorted bad habits. My life lacked direction.

Absenting myself from classes for a few days, I hitched two hundred miles to visit my sister in South Wales – a perilous journey for one so innocent. She was studying at Swansea University, and I landed on her doorstep in the week preceding final examinations. However, she took me in with great kindness and understanding, none of which I appreciated at the time. I passed several important milestones during the brief period of my stay, although at the time I was unaware that between them they would stake out the perimeter of my future. The most significant event was that I was taken rock climbing.

A visit to the Gower coast with the college climbing club had been promised from the outset. It was an exciting proposition, although I knew nothing of what to expect. True I had done some fell walking in the Lake District, but oddly enough had no recollection of the cliffs and climbers I must have seen. What had impressed me more were the stories Jenny told about her climbing adventures. I was very proud of her and doubted that anyone else in the country – let alone the school – could boast a sister who had once fallen down a crevasse in an Alpine glacier. What troubled my mind as we caught the bus out of town was the tenuous link between the Alps and the Three Cliffs. Was it really possible that somewhere on a nearby beach, mixed up with bikinis and ice-creams, there would be cliffs worthy of the attention of real climbers? I feared a deception, but went along anyway.

The cliffs were real enough. As we rounded the headland three huge fins of rock came into view, rising from the sands as if some great prehistoric beast lay buried there. A tremendous feeling of excitement welled up inside me. I wanted to rush across to the rocks and begin climbing at once, except that I did not know how to climb. Instead, I laced up my corduroy beach shoes, feigned indifference and waited patiently for the adventure to begin.

The club had enough rope for just two groups of climbers, and those places had already been claimed. Some of those who had tied on appeared unwilling to start and were obviously inventing excuses for the delay – fiddling with knots, cleaning boot soles, arranging equipment. This seemed a terrible injustice when set against my own eagerness. I was choking with frustration. Jenny clearly understood my condition (or had seen an opportunity to rid herself of a pesky brother) and proposed that we should climb unroped. I agreed at once. She urged me to follow her movements precisely, to test each handhold carefully and, above all, not to fall off. Then we began.

At first we moved easily over sea-scoured lower rocks, Jenny climbing nimbly in bare feet despite flesh ripping encrustations of shells. Soon the cliff reared up into a wall of bubbly rock. So futile did the direct attempt appear that I guessed we would find an easy way around, but Jenny moved on to the steeper rock without a pause, her hands and feet moving over its surface without hesitation. My trust in her was total; I also moved on to the steepening face.

By now the tide had turned and the first tongues of water were licking the lowest rocks. The sound of cheerful banter passing between the other climbers drowned in the waves which thumped and sloshed through the natural arch in the cliff base. I doubted the possibility of retreat. 'Don't look down', Jenny said. But, gripped by curiosity, I *did* look down: down beyond shoes half supported on a narrow ledge; down beyond folds of rock already climbed. I expected to be frightened, but instead was exhilarated. To be poised between earth and sky – neither moving nor staying, secure nor falling – seemed to me to be the most wonderful sensation imaginable.

Whenever I moved, patches of rock would, in turn, enlarge in vision and snap into sharp focus. If one contained no usable hold, it would blur and shrink back into the mass while another was selected and searched. If this new patch revealed a hold a hand would dart up and settle there, its fingers nestling into the indentations. At some synchronised signal the body would tighten and lean, a foot extending across the wall to maintain balance. With each move made, another search would begin. I wished it would go on for ever.

Quite suddenly I realised that we had climbed to within a few metres of the summit. With the goal now in sight I only wanted it all to be over, to sit exultant on the topmost rock and look down on people small as ants scurrying from the incoming tide, to pity them for their lowly situation. Although the climbing had become much easier, some of the holds rattled alarmingly in their sockets like rotten teeth. I knew I must be very careful not to rush and make a mistake. How ironic that would be! Muscles tensed so that I began to move in jerks like a teetering wooden doll, lunging for holds and committing my weight to them without prior test. A vision flashed through my mind of a body surging in and out of the sea arch on a rising tide . . .

My recollection ends there. Oddly enough I cannot remember reaching the top – my first real summit – although we must have passed over it in order to reach safety on the grass slopes beyond. Our arrival on top must have seemed an anticlimax after the experiences below.

I am not suggesting that my own initiation to rock climbing was in any way typical or laudable, but I count myself fortunate in being able to look back on it with such profound happiness. I have never relinquished or renounced the sensations I experienced on my first climb, however naive they might seem in retrospect. In fact, I suspect I have been subconsciously trying to recreate them in all my subsequent adventures, and to this day I take special delight in climbing unroped.

Your first experience of climbing will certainly be very different from mine, but I sincerely hope that it will engage the true spirit of the sport in some way. If you have yet to touch rock I would urge you to make that first encounter in the company of friends, relatives, or club acquaintances – even if later you choose to learn the rudiments of ropework with a paid instructor. This first 'climb' need not be a recognised route; it could be a steep rise in a gully scramble, or a toppled boulder below cliffs. What matters is that you make the effort of your own volition, not through a sense of duty when fifth in line at the end of an instructor's rope.

This story has an epilogue. A few years ago I returned to the Gower in the hope of rediscovering my roots. I suppose I ought to have known better. The Three Cliffs, now appearing as unimpressive lumps in the sand, did not seem at all familiar. Holiday-makers lounged in beach chairs at their foot while I scrambled up and down the rocks trying, unsuccessfully as it turned out, to find some feature that would remind me of where I had gone all those years before. While searching, I was distracted by an impressively smooth slab of rock which cut across the roof of a natural arch. It would make an excellent climb.

The rock was steep right from the start and after a few upward moves I thought about going down. But something took hold of me and I found myself going on – reaching, pulling, swaying – until before long I stepped on to some tiny footholds above the arch itself. On this occasion it was low water, so the tide which surged through the tunnel beneath was one of people. Some of them paused to look up at me for a few seconds, surprised or curious, before continuing to where they had left towels and suntan lotion. For a moment I felt ridiculous perched up there above their heads, clinging to a lump of rock and a fading memory, but the climb had become an absorbing one and in need of all my concentration if I was to succeed. Locking my fingertips into the creases, I kicked up with taut muscles towards the summit. The movement rekindled an old memory. I wished it would go on for ever.

2 First Climbs

What a difference the rope makes! It shows that you mean business, that you have outgrown 'mere' scrambling and now seek real trouble (don't worry – you'll find it). Of course, this new status bars you from further fraternisation with non-climbers; not that you would find anything they had to say to be of the slightest interest! Instead you should remain silent and aloof and adopt the grim expression of a mountaineer closing with his fate . . .

It was my first telegram: 'Meet M6/A5 Friday 9 p.m. for Wales', it said, 'Bring boots and butties. Tony.' I felt very important. This was the long-awaited summons from my brother. He had a rope; this would be the real thing. I searched the hall cupboard for a pair of hiking boots that might pass for proper climbing boots – hard luck if they happened to be three sizes too big!

Our lifts from opposite ends of the country dropped us at a windswept Cannock Chase within five minutes of each other. Tony wore his army combat gear; I made do with my school anorak and mountaineer's expression. We travelled to Wales together and asked our driver to put us down on the crest of a bleak pass. Rain lashed against the windscreen. All we could see in the headlights were stone walls and a fallen telephone line thrashing in the wind. We watched the rear lights blur and disappear into the night before turning down the farm track.

Voiceless stares shone back at us in the torch beam as we flung open the barn door. In each straw-filled pit nestled a pair of climbers, cosy in their sleeping bags. No vacancies. We found a thinly padded shelf and wrapped ourselves up, wet and shivering, in our blankets. I fell asleep listening to the scratching of rats among the rafters.

We awoke to the drumming of rain on the roof tiles. An enticing aroma penetrated the blankets – fried bacon. Peering down, we watched the early risers hunched goblin-like over roaring paraffin stoves. For some reason they appeared in no rush to leave. We pulled on boots, ate half our stock of beef paste sandwiches, and set off for the hills.

A film of water rippled over the rock, bloating pads of lichen into slippery sponges. Rain soaked our clothes until they hung from our shoulders like wash rags. My fingers had turned white with cold. Tony pointed to a sinister groove; probably the drainage downpipe for that part of the crag. A small waterfall issued from its base. 'We'll climb that' he said, arranging the rope around my waist and hands in the prescribed manner. He kicked each boot against the rock to dislodge mud from the soles and then set off up the groove in optimistic mood. I thought it all very exciting.

At first Tony made reasonable progress by pulling himself up on small spikes of rock and resting between times by wedging himself in the angle of the groove. The spikes got smaller and smaller until, at about housetop height, they

Climbs and Climbers

disappeared altogether. Now he was reduced to a sort of fast pedalling motion with his feet. I assumed this to be an accepted technique on these harder climbs. Evidently I was wrong. To his credit he kept his dignity to the last and let go without a squeak, but events were beyond his control after that and he rumbled down the groove towards me like a sack in a coal chute. The rope hung limp in my arms; obviously I could do nothing to help him so instead I sought to help myself. I jumped aside at the last moment, leaving his way clear to fetch up spread-eagled over a boulder at my feet. He emitted a long, low groan. I assumed this sort of thing often happened so tried not to make a fuss. Fortunately Tony was merely winded and was soon on his feet again. He made a spirited attempt to re-enter the groove, having read somewhere that a fallen leader risked losing his nerve unless he immediately re-addressed the rock. However, I pointed out that the climb was probably beyond me and he graciously agreed to postpone the attempt. We retreated to the barn for a second breakfast of beef paste.

Among other things, this first experience of roped climbing taught us that we could not fall off with impunity. I suppose our youthful exuberance had got the better of us. In fact, we had made not one but several mistakes: poor choice of route, misuse of equipment, ignorance of conditions, wrong assessment of difficulties and inadequate preparation. Heaven help us had we got any higher up the cliff! I would not wish this traumatic experience on any beginner, and yet we must all learn from mistakes. What I would suggest is that you use other people's mistakes to learn from – it is much less painful. Ideally, you should at least try to understand the fundamentals of rope protection, its applications and limitations, before you reach neck-breaking height on a big cliff. Later chapters have the details.

Finding someone to take you climbing may not be easy. Unless someone is known to you personally, your best alternative might be to join a local climbing club. Magazines listed in the bibliography include the addresses of club secretaries. Additionally some schools and most colleges will support clubs of their own, often with an equipment pool of specialised items such as ropes, helmets and harnesses. Joining a club has

Fig 2   Pulpit Route, Milestone Buttress.

First Climbs

advantages beyond those of securing partners, borrowing equipment and sharing transport costs. Most importantly of all, you will make lasting friendships with people who share your enthusiasm for climbing.

A second alternative is to enrol on a climbing course organised by an outdoor activities centre or qualified guide. You will receive expert tuition on ropework and might find yourself climbing difficult routes by the end of the week. For all that, however, the professional environment is an unnatural one and certainly no long-term substitute for regular climbing partners.

Fig 3 Young people attending an Outdoor Centre climbing course.

I have to admit that I never joined a club or went on a climbing course when I began climbing (although I have since been associated with both in various capacities). Instead, having survived our violent encounter with the water-washed groove, my brother and I taught ourselves the basic techniques which we then applied with great caution. As a consequence, our progress up the ladder of difficulty was very slow indeed; some five years elapsed before we felt ready to lead *Extreme* grade routes, and we never did climb the hardest routes of the day. There are no regrets, though, because we have had the satisfaction of making each new discovery for ourselves.

It could be that your first climb takes place on a small outcrop no more than ten metres high, in which case it will not be necessary to regroup on midway ledges as you would on a bigger cliff. Instead, the leader will climb straight to the top in one go. Ropework will be straightforward and there will be few communication problems. In fact, you can still climb even if no one is willing or capable of leading. What happens is that someone will gain the top of the climb by finding an easy scramble to one side. He will then lower down the rope end for each climber to tie on and ascend in turn. The method is called *top roping* and allows all members of the party to receive the full protection of the rope. It is particularly useful when climbing on unreliable rock, such as soft sandstone. However, top roping is not generally used in other circumstances because it bypasses the uncertainty of the lead – an intangible and possibly romantic concept which lies at the heart of the sport's traditions.

Everyone begins by seconding, only

Climbs and Climbers

later progressing to sharing the lead. The role of the second is a vital one, since without proper rope handling and moral support even the most able leader cannot function. That is why all roped climbs are undertaken as partnerships, although this is something you may not appreciate at first. Eventually you will come to realise that it is the whole enterprise which is important, not just a daring individual lead. So never consider yourself a passenger on a climb, however expert your companions. Enjoyment of both the climb and the day will depend on you as much as anyone else.

Tony and I attempted our first 'big' climb twelve months after that first outing. That night in the barn (the same one, although we now had the luxury of stove, food and sleeping bags!) we agonised over the decision for hours. Grooved Arete was a famous classic climb on the 250m high East Face of Tryfan – a wonderful rocky peak dominating the Ogwen Valley in Snowdonia. It would be our most difficult climb to date. This time we were better prepared. Our equipment, although still fairly primitive, was at least adequate, and we were more fully aware of its potential and limitations. More importantly, we had bought a guidebook which told us the location of good climbs and how difficult we might expect them to be. On the traditional and somewhat archaic grading scale (still in use), Grooved Arete rated *Hard Very Difficult*. In everyday climbing parlance this translates as 'fairly easy', although as comparative beginners we were certain to be taxed to our limit.

I could not get to sleep that night. What if we met impossible difficulties high on the cliff, perhaps on the Knight's Slab

Fig 4 Poor Man's Peuterey, one of the classic Severes at Tremadog.

which the guidebook had described in such sinister terms? If I slipped from its diagonal traverse I might swing beyond help into unknown grooves. The whole prospect filled me with an unsettling mixture of longing and trepidation. Eventually I fell asleep exhausted with anxiety.

We awoke to a fine summer's day, the morning rays falling obliquely on the mountain so that even at this distance we could pick out the line of our route.

All Tryfan's East Face climbs begin from a terrace which slants across the face – that would be our first objective. We followed a narrow path which zigzagged up a heather slope and entered a stone-filled runnel. Impatient for the real climb-

First Climbs

Fig 5   The crux of Murray's Route, Dow Crag.

ing, we rushed straight up a tongue of unstable rocks thinking it to be the path. In fact, it was a scree run used only in descent. We wasted a great deal of energy on it.

The terrace itself is a remarkable feature; you might mistake it for an ancient trackway cut across the mountainside. We joined a straggling caravan which was already making its way along. In front and behind, small groups of people toiled against the slope and the hot sun. At intervals they would cast off their burden of rope and rucksack and fling themselves down in a panting heap at the foot of their chosen climb, making a great show of being glad to have the walking part over and done with. We did likewise at the foot of Grooved Arete, allowing ourselves a slightly superior smirk because it happened to be one of the harder climbs. Ours was none the less a popular climb, so Tony insisted we sat at its very foot to prevent late comers from sneaking in before us.

Tony placed a sling over a flake of rock while I uncoiled the rope. This anchor would secure me to the rock while I belayed. Nervous but excited, I payed out rope a few centimetres at a time while Tony worked his way up the first awkward fissure. Twenty metres higher he gained a room-sized ledge, passed a sling over the top of a large block and secured himself to it with a length of rope. Now that Tony was secure I released the belay so he could pull in the spare rope between us. A few moments later it tightened at my waist – no going back now. I was eager to start but had to wait until he called for me to climb before removing my own anchor sling and making ready to begin.

Once I had started climbing I forgot about the increasing drop below my feet and concentrated on making the best use of holds. Tony had shouted down a few suggestions, but it was pointless trying to remember precisely which holds he had used. Instead I worked out each problem for myself, safeguarded throughout by the rope which Tony drew in – neither tight nor slack – to match my every upward move. Our reunion at the ledge jolted us from private reveries.

We encountered our first real trial at the twin grooves. The guidebook had warned us to expect some precarious climbing, but Tony was still surprised by the smoothness of it all. From my stance below and to one side I could see little of what was happening, but could judge by erratic rope movements and an occasional grunt that the climbing was difficult. Moments later Tony bobbed into view, quite high now, with a wild look in his eye. He appeared to be searching for something and twitched with rodent-like urgency. The fact that a slip would result in a twenty-metre fall on to broken rocks might have had something to do with it. Eventually he found what he was looking for – protection. With some strain he held on with one hand while threading a sling through a small hole in the rock; there was a good deal of swearing before he succeeded. Joining the two ends of the sling together with a karabiner, he clipped in his rope and let out a great sigh of relief. So did I. Provided the sling held firm, a slip now would result in a fall of only a few metres – twice the distance he happened to be above this 'runner' at the time. With this reassurance he completed the pitch without further hesitation.

When my turn came to follow I feared I might need a pull on the rope to help me over the difficult part. Instead I was surprised to find the groove quite straightforward and I reached Tony's threaded sling without difficulty. I removed the sling, placed it over my shoulders and proceeded up what I thought would be an easy finish. How wrong I was! I landed on the ledge with a gasp, much to Tony's amusement, and acknowledged his good lead of the pitch.

The slender 'grooved arete' itself rose above us now in a single majestic sweep, knifing into the huge black tower which dominated this part of the face. Unknown difficulties lay ahead; we could not relax. We ate lunch and looked down on some tiny figures, rucksacks bobbing on their backs, as they inched their way up the terrace in the full heat of the afternoon sun. We were in shade and, at an altitude of 800m, conscious of a cold edge to the wind. By now the valley bottom was so far below us that it no longer seemed part of this chaotic world of rock.

The grooved arete surrendered without a struggle – apart from one occasion when it tricked Tony into going too high. Misled by an ambiguity in the guidebook description, he was forced to reverse down a few metres (always harder than going up) until he could rejoin the correct route leading to the Haven.

For some reason I felt deeply anxious at

Fig 6   Problem solving on Merlin, a Tremadog VS.

the Haven. Here we were, I thought, trapped on some God-forsaken ledge in the middle of a huge cliff, probably unable to retreat down the last pitch and unlikely to get up the next, the notorious Knight's Slab. Historical notes in the guidebook told of a fatality here: imagine some poor climber slithering from his holds and plunging into the abyss. We should never have attempted the stupid climb; was it really worth it? I vowed never to go climbing again!

Such is the power of imagination and reputation. In fact, we climbed the Knight's Slab without undue difficulty. It was a relief to discover that it possessed any holds at all! Tony grinned down at me as I discovered for myself the key sequence which led intricately but securely up and across the chessboard slab.

This stance was tiny in comparison to all preceding ones – no bigger than a hall table. Engrossed in safely swapping anchors we had failed to notice the cloud now swirling around us, threatening damp and drizzle. If we had felt apprehensive at the Haven, we ought now to have felt terrified on this perch so dramatically set above an awesome drop. It induced precisely the opposite feeling – we had nothing to lose! Our confidence in each other was absolute. Nothing was going to stop us now; neither the cloud nor the rain nor the slippery rocks, not even the evil looking corner which rose above our heads and promised a grim struggle. The rope buzzed with the power and the certainty of what we were doing.

Nothing did stop us. Before long we had coiled the rope above the final pitch and had begun scrambling up easy rocks to the summit. I was filled with an indescribable joy. It had not been easy, but nowhere had we climbed recklessly. We had crossed a major threshold in our climbing careers and could now gaze upon the ocean of new possibilities which stretched before us.

3 Leading

Enthusiastic beginners usually aspire to share the lead on their climbs. The reasons for this are diverse, ranging from simple curiosity through to visions of death or glory. Whatever the motivation, there is no doubt that leading adds depth to the climbing experience.

My own chance to lead came six months after our graduation on Grooved Arete. Ogwen, our usual haunt, would have welcomed us gladly, but as climbers of ambition we felt obliged to seek out grim surroundings to match our grim expressions. The Llanberis Pass was in gloomy mood that bleak December day as we negotiated its bends on my overladen motorcycle. At either side a scree littered hillside swept down at an ugly angle to meet its opposing slope in the sunless V of the valley base. Small cliffs studded the northern slope, their vertical faces gathering up a few scraps of winter sunlight. Among them was Carreg Wastad, an unusually compact crag rippled by apparently unstable flutings. We stopped to admire its central feature, a jutting prow undercut by a band of overhangs. This was Crackstone Rib, our number one objective in the Pass. Neither of us had actually seen the route before, although we had been exposed to so many photographic evocations of the climb (silhouettes being the preferred treatment) that this made no difference.

The cliff was deserted, gripped by cold – just like us. We uncoiled the rope in silence. Tony handed me a rope end: 'Your lead', he said, ignoring my gasp of astonishment. Evidently he had planned this for me all along.

The climbing began with a runnel polished smooth by the passage of thousands of boot soles. Down it trickled a vein of water, spoiling what little remained of foot friction. Self-confidence ebbed away. Tony waited patiently a few metres below while I discovered the problems of fixing runners. Eventually I succeeded in lodging one of our few nut runners in the crack and resumed the ascent with renewed courage. Unfortunately my boot caught in the sling as I stepped up. The nut rattled down the rope on its karabiner and slid into Tony's waiting hand. Furious at my incompetence I flung myself at the rock, heaving and pulling on holds which might easily have given way under my weight. It was a reckless performance.

Momentum carried me on to a steeper face, but in my haste I had failed to notice the rock spike at its foot which would have taken a reliable sling runner. Now I was stuck. I rapidly became frightened as I clung to my small finger holds and wondered what to do next. I searched for somewhere to place a runner, but could find no crack or flake in the compact rock. Jagged rocks waited below. Leading was no fun after all, I decided.

Slowly, I began to climb back down the wall. Tony offered encouragement and pointed out holds as best he could, but really it was a personal struggle. Although I was terrified and on the brink of panic, my limbs seemed to be doing all

Leading

the right things. A flood of relief swept over me when finally I stepped down on to a ledge below the wall. Back in control, I placed a sling over the spike and clipped in the rope. Tony looked worried – as well he might – and asked if I was prepared to continue. However, with the runner fixed I felt much happier and nodded my intentions; with its protection the traverse seemed effortless. A few minutes later I arrived at a tiny ledge adjacent to the rib.

While self-consciously mumbling the unfamiliar leader's calls I anchored to a cluster of spikes, drew in the slack rope and made ready to belay. Secretly I hoped someone might pass below the crag and look up wondering who this bold and capable leader at work on Crackstone Rib might be. But only Tony saw me, and he was not so easily impressed. All the same, it was thrilling to trace the arc of rope where it crossed the wall below and marvel at the fact that I had climbed up there protected by nothing more than a crotchety spike.

Tony brought me down to earth. With his fist he thumped the anchor spikes to demonstrate their looseness. Then he complained that the securing loop was too slack. Finally he criticised my choice of body position, implying that had he fallen I would have been pulled off my feet, probably letting go of the rope. My pride was dented. Why was he trying to spoil everything? 'But you didn't fall,' I protested. 'No, not this time,' was all he said. Of course, he was right. After putting everything in order he moved out on to the tiny holds of the rib and began climbing skywards, silhouetted by the afternoon sun. Just like the pictures.

The leader's role extends far beyond that of accepting the possibility of a longer fall. There are the extra responsibilities of route finding, of making stances secure, and of safeguarding the second during traverses. The rewards are also proportionately greater; not least that of being first to solve obstacles encountered on the route. Leading is the rock climbing equivalent of driving in the fast lane.

Fortunately, my supervised lead of Crackstone Rib exposed me to the immediate sensation and personal danger of leading without having to accept overall responsibility. Three months elapsed before I felt ready to lead a less experienced companion on a climb.

The decision making process began

Fig 7   Nearing the top of Bramble Buttress, a satisfying VDiff climb at Tremadog.

long before travelling to Wales. Dave had already agreed in principle to come climbing for the weekend, provided we would not be attempting anything too difficult. I needed to find a route which would prove exciting without taxing our limited experience. I borrowed some guidebooks to the area and began to study them closely.

I was tempted by some of the long climbs at Idwal and Lliwedd, but being early March we would risk encountering damp rock on their sunless faces. Besides, the air temperature at seven or eight hundred metres would be several degrees below what we might expect in the valleys. South facing cliffs at Tremadog promised an interesting day, but a glance through the guide revealed few good climbs at a grade we might realistically attempt. Eventually I found what I was looking for – a climb called Flying Buttress on Dinas Cromlech in the Llanberis Pass. The cliff faced south, carried little drainage from the hillside above and could be reached from the road with a twenty-minute walk. Moreover, the guide described the route in glowing terms: 'a classic at the grade' (an amenable *Difficult*), it said, and awarded a maximum three stars for overall quality and interest. It had six pitches, none of them very long, promising plenty of variety. In the climb's 100m length there were ridges, pinnacles, exposed traverses, and – to keep us guessing to the end – an awkward chimney to finish.

The next day I approached Dave with the proposition, carefully playing down the difficulties mentioned in the guide – he was at a disadvantage since I contrived to leave the guidebook at home! Infected by my enthusiasm he agreed. I surreptitiously repossessed the guidebook and we left for Wales.

Dinas Cromlech towered above as we clattered up a slope of unstable scree. An open-book feature at its centre dominated our upward view whenever we paused for breath. This was Cenotaph Corner, the most famous climb in Britain. It looked holdless and impossibly steep; if someone had suggested then that I would climb it one day, I would have thought them insane. In comparison, the notched ridge of Flying Buttress which defined the right side of the crag, and towards which we now turned, looked to be little more than a scramble.

Dave seemed reluctant to anchor himself below the first pitch. He saw little point in it, he said, considering I could hardly fall further than the ground. I

Fig 8 Contemplating the difficult slab on New West Climb, a classic Diff on Pillar Rock.

related an incident which took place the week before: a leader almost tugged from his holds by a restless second who had tripped over a boulder while wandering about at the foot of the crag. He took the point and fixed an anchor – one less worry.

The holds were large but polished, the climbing more difficult than we had been led to expect. Towards the end of the pitch the ridge steepened into a wall. Recalling the Crackstone Rib episode, I fixed a good runner before relinquishing my position of relative comfort on easier rocks. This would be my insurance if I failed to locate a runner on the wall itself. As a result I arrived on the first belay ledge still feeling in control. In his turn Dave climbed the pitch with ease, his long reach demolishing the few difficult moves. I suppressed a desire to see him struggle just a little.

The upper half of the ridge presented no major obstacles. I fixed a sling runner around one of the crenellations at its top and descended into the notch beyond. By now, however, the rope had passed between so many pinnacles that it was in danger of jamming. Even with two hands I could barely pull it through. Besides, I realised that Dave would not have the full protection of the rope while climbing down to join me in the notch. There was nothing for it but to climb back up to the crest and take my belay stance there.

Concerned by the delay Dave began calling up to me, but his words were muffled by the wind. Fearing a reply might be misinterpreted and lead to yet more confusion, I remained silent and concentrated instead on arranging the anchors. Once I had pulled up all the slack rope and arranged the belay, I gave three sharp tugs on the rope to indicate that he could begin climbing – our pre-arranged signal if communication proved difficult. After his confirming reply of three tugs I felt the rope come slack as he began to climb. We were back in business. A few minutes later he passed by and 'led' the few metres down into the notch to occupy the next stance.

The mood changed. Having left behind the friendly ridge and its comforting holds we now contemplated the imposing walls of the upper buttress. A bitterly cold wind funnelled through the notch, further eroding our confidence. According to the guidebook the best climbing was yet to come, and I felt sure our spirits

Fig 9 The traverse on Pedestal Route, a popular VDiff at the Roaches.

Fig 10 Eliminate 'C', a VS on Dow Crag.

Fig 11 Lavaredo Wall, Carreg Alltrem. Large holds compensate for the verticality on this exposed VS.

would rise once we got to grips with it, but Dave muttered something about 'giving it best' and pointed to what looked like an easy escape route on to scree at the side of the cliff. 'I'll just try the first few moves,' I said, 'and if it proves at all difficult I'll come back down.' Of course, I had not the slightest intention of coming down. 'It's all right', I said, trying my best to make some awkward moves in a groove appear straightforward. Dave looked unconvinced but seemed resigned to his fate. The ruse had worked; we would go on.

An impressively situated traverse now led out leftwards to a ledge on the buttress front. Eager to reach it, I was tempted to begin the traverse at once, but then I realised that from my stance the rope would slant diagonally across to Dave while he tackled the difficult groove. Even a minor slip would develop into an appalling pendulum swing across the wall. If I placed a runner immediately above the groove, I reasoned, Dave would have the reassurance of rope protection from above. I placed the runner, clipped it to the rope and traversed easily across to the stance.

We felt vulnerable perched on our exposed ledge, with the wind gusting around us and unknown difficulties lurking above. With exaggerated care we exchanged positions so that Dave could belay my rope while I explored the next pitch. A few snowflakes began to fall, brushing dryly against the cold rock. I feared for our morale and dared not mention them. I stepped up as if to begin but then faltered. What if I took the wrong route and climbed into yet greater difficulties? What if the snowfall worsened and began coating the footholds? What if . . .? I glanced down towards the boulder bed fifty metres below, but Dave's encouraging smile interrupted my line of sight. 'You'll be all right,' he said, motioning me to continue, the rope gripped firm in his hands.

As it happened, I had no choice but to follow the correct line. Smooth rock bulged above, forcing me to climb to the right across a slanting gangway. In ordinary circumstances the passage would have been simple, but my fingers were white with cold and I could no longer feel the texture of the rock. With agonising slowness I teetered across and clambered on to a broad ledge. For five minutes I crouched helpless, sobbing like a child from the pain of blood flowing back into my hands.

I guessed Dave would appreciate some moral support in return; instead of tying directly to the belay anchors – which would have placed me out of sight – I extended their securing loops so that I could stand overlooking the gangway. Finally I placed a subsidiary anchor immediately above to improve stability of the system. Now I could watch Dave's every move and offer encouragement should it become necessary.

'You didn't tell me about this,' Dave said, looking up at the chimney which barred us from the top. Dave hated chimneys, but the weather was getting worse and daylight had begun to fade – we had no option. I threw myself at the horrible fissure, determined to settle the issue one way or another. Almost at once my foot slipped and I slithered back on to the ledge. Dave said nothing. Our situation was fast becoming serious. I tried again, scrabbling with my knees, but it was no use and I flopped back down. Defeated by a *Diff* ! The ignominy of it! Dave calmly pointed to a foothold which I had failed to notice in my haste. It was not much of a hold, but it would do. With its help I attained a tenable position in the chimney and wriggled up to better holds. I could smell success, but the rock was streaked with drainage water so I forced myself to place a final runner as disaster insurance.

Dave arrived red in the face, his distaste of chimneys confirmed, but he was obviously delighted with the climb. We spoke in loud voices, reliving each incident of the climb. It was *our* climb, *our* day, and we were determined to wring from it every last drop of mutual credit. You would think we had climbed Cenotaph Corner the way we strutted into the barn that night.

4 Boulders and Training

Try to define rock climbing as a single, all-embracing concept and you risk tying yourself in philosophical knots. Instead, your conception of the sport should grow from what you do in its name, and nowadays that is increasingly likely to include fringe activities such as bouldering, indoor wall climbing and even strength training.

The term *bouldering* collectively describes unroped attempts on miniature climbs. These might be found on small outcrops, at the base of larger crags, or on fallen boulders found beneath either. Some famous problems find their way into guidebooks, their appeal and stature enhanced by notoriety, whereas the majority – charming in their anonymity – await individual rediscovery.

Novices sometimes despise bouldering as 'mere play', whereas the majority of climbers recognise its true worth – not simply as training for bigger things, useful though it is for that purpose, but as an end in itself. Unencumbered by ropes and other paraphernalia, some regard bouldering as the purest form of climbing.

I count several boulder problems among my favourite climbs. Whereas I have difficulty recalling the events of some of my Alpine routes, I can relive each micro-second of these cameo experiences. Unconvinced? By nature, this facet of rock climbing evokes obscure and emotive description, but hopefully this plain account of a typical problem will help to establish a proper context for this fascinating game.

Attractively sculptured, the boulder stands three metres from the track. Over the years I have passed this place a dozen times, but in my impatience for bigger climbs I have failed to notice its potential until now. A six-metre wall slices its right side, not quite vertical but apparently holdless. From its top a tantalising fingertip flake extends downwards for one metre. This will be the objective.

Close examination reveals a surface to the rock that is rippled like sand exposed by an ebbing tide. The rock itself is of medium texture, promising good friction for boot soles on the protruding lower edges of the ripples. So much for the clinical inspection. In real terms the wall will be almost impossible for me to climb – the perfect boulder problem. It begins to rain before I have so much as laid a finger on it; but I can wait.

A few days later I return armed with a bag of chalk and a cotton rag; the chalk is for drying sweaty fingertips, the rag for drying muddy boot soles after each failed attempt.

I have no concept of time passing. Five attempts and an undetermined number of minutes later I have solved the problem of how to stand on the first hold with my right foot. Progress. Unfortunately my arms are spread in a crucifix position, held there by fingertips which grip the sharp edges of cornflake-sized holds. I can see a hold for the left foot, but each time I attempt to place it the slight shift in balance causes the right foot to slither from its precarious position. I try again, this time leaning my body to the right and ignoring the screaming pain in overloaded fingers. This movement appears to delay my downward departure by about three seconds. This might be enough.

The next attempt wins the elusive left foothold. I transfer my full weight to it and straighten. Now I am leaning against the wall while supported purely by one foot placed sideways on its three millimetre edge. I am so excited by this partial success that I fall off. The distance to the ground is one metre. Three times I repeat the opening manoeuvre; three times without success. On the fourth attempt the cruel cornflake rips the pad of hard skin from my left middle fingertip and puts an end to the campaign; but I will return.

For two months the problem lies dormant while I am distracted by bigger climbs and by mundane matters. A spare hour one fine evening rekindles the memory. In the interim rain has washed from the finger holds all traces of white chalk. With crab-like hands I begin searching the rock for the correct combination. Suddenly it feels right; at once I step up, make the transfer left, and straighten – all in one fluid movement as if the choreography has programmed itself into my muscles during earlier attempts. With finger strength in reserve I have a few seconds to explore the next move before my foot creeps from its hold.

Despairing of finding a handhold I simply stand up on a poor friction hold to see what happens. It stays! I have a small chance of success. Unable to reach the fingertip flake, I repeat the previous manoeuvre by stepping up on the sloping lower lip of one of the ripples, hands pawing the rock to aid stability. Now I can just touch the lower extremity of the flake. What a disappointment; barely half a fingertip will tuck behind it. For the flake to be of any use I must lean backwards and work my feet higher up the rock. If my fingers choose that moment to uncurl I will topple over and hit the ground on my back. I consider cutting my losses by jumping off to a possible twisted ankle but instead, intuitively, decide to go on. I sense a shiver of excitement as the commitment is made. The torment of indecision has lasted about three seconds. Now I need to prepare, mentally and physically. In turn I release each hand and dab my fingers into the chalk bag strung behind my back – a ritual act equivalent to the high diver's final breath before springing from the board. Once resettled, the dry grip feels much more secure.

I have made no conscious decision to initiate the sequence but now find myself leaning backwards and swaying to one side. The tension in my fingers increases as I raise the right foot and place it flat against the rock where it is held secure by its grainy texture. The flake edge bites reassuringly into my fingertip pads as I work them a few centimetres higher. At this moment my left foot skids from its hold, the change in equilibrium having deprived it of retaining pressure. Slowly I begin to pivot outwards like a door on oiled hinges. If I do nothing, then in less than two seconds I will pass the mechanical threshold beyond which my fingers will peel from their holds.

With nothing to lose I lean back further, raise the errant foot and jab it against the rock. It stays. Immediately I raise the

Climbs and Climbers

other foot, kicking it far out to the right in the hope of finally restoring balance. Magically it finds a good hold for itself. My head pounds, but I dare not pause to reflect on the fleeting sensations which flicker and die there like images in a fire. My strength is fading. With a final lurch I pull into an upright position, defying the physics of friction, and claw over the top for some kind of finishing hold; anything will do.

I am astonished to find myself heaving over on a pathetic little edge, wrists quivering at the strain. It places me safe on the flat top of the boulder. For an instant I remain crouched and tense, like a cat about to spring. In my entire existence I have never felt so alive as this.

TRAINING

Bouldering at its best takes place when you desire to climb the problems for their own sakes, but it is none the less true that the training aspect of the game acts as a valid incentive. A one-hour bouldering session is equivalent to a hundred metres of high standard roped climbing, so improvements in finger strength and mental agility can be tremendous. Those benefits notwithstanding, an emphasis on dynamics will encourage the boulderer to neglect the skills and stamina required for leading difficult rock, when the ability to rest between sequences or when placing runners becomes as important as the abil-

Fig 12 Brownstones Quarry, an ideal bouldering venue near Bolton, Lancashire.

ity to complete the actual moves. One way to make good this deficiency is to simulate longer climbs by traversing the base of the outcrop – if necessary three or four times in succession without touching ground. As you begin to tire you will seek out all manner of contorted rest positions in which to relieve the agony of aching muscles.

A familiar bouldering venue is best for training purposes. That way you will spend a greater proportion of your time on rock than otherwise. Boredom from repetition is not the problem it seems because good bouldering involves stimulating, dance-like movements. A useful training circuit will include perhaps a dozen five-metre problems ranging from slabs to overhanging cracks. Interest will be maintained if you can end the session with attempts on an inspiring, if perhaps impossible, 'last great problem'.

The tangible benefits of bouldering can be dramatic. A *VDiff* climber, for example, can sample (and probably succeed on) any amount of *VS* climbing during a couple of bouldering sessions. That knowledge will subsequently prove to be of immense value when exploring routes of a new standard of difficulty. Not surprisingly, it becomes harder to make substantial improvements as you progress further up the grading scale. Instead, climbers who have 'peaked' in terms of technical ability will use boulder training as a means of quickly getting fit and 'thinking rock' after a winter lay-off.

Not everyone is fortunate in living close to a natural outcrop. Alternative venues include stone buildings, bridge embankments and other man-made structures. Some of these sites have had guidebooks written for them! Repetitive climbing and a lack of interesting features would be a major drawback were it not for the ingenuity of frustrated climbers in creating bizarre problems from unpromising raw material.

Wall Training

Another alternative turns the 'buildering' idea inside out to give the purpose-built indoor climbing wall. The recent proliferation of these structures indicates the degree of importance now attributed to regular training by those who aspire to technical excellence. Wall design varies tremendously, not only in the construction of holds but in overall concept. Many consist of a single vertical wall, whereas a more ambitious design will also include overhangs, cracks, slabs and other realistic features.

Indoor walls generally make poor substitutes for genuine outcrops when introducing newcomers to the sport. Not only do they lack the atmosphere of outdoor rock, but the climbing lacks its variety. Besides, the move sequences are invariably too strenuous and difficult for a complete beginner to cope with. Some walls have the facility for rope protection, but most climbers prefer to concentrate on short problems or low level traverses. In this sense the wall is being used as an all-weather bouldering venue. Exceptions include crag-like outdoor structures where routes may be led in the conventional manner. The usefulness of a wall depends as much on its administration as its design. Restrictions such as time limits, compulsory use of ropes, and a ban on chalk, all detract from the value of the facility.

Intensive and regular use of indoor

Fig 13

Fig 14

Fig 15

Fig 16 A 'heel hook' solves this exciting boulder problem (a meadow of soft grass, just out of picture, awaits the unsuccessful!)

Boulders and Training

walls (i.e. several hours per week, every week) has produced some dramatic individual improvements. There are well-known cases of moderate climbers being catapulted to the forefront of technical achievement after emerging from a winter of wall training. In this application the climber will use the wall to develop finger strength, endurance, and the mental agility to suppress debilitating anxiety in order to solve highly technical problems. However, over-enthusiasm can lead to troublesome and persistent injuries to muscles, tendons and ligaments. Some very good climbers have been forced into premature retirement for this reason.

Exercise

In addition to wall training, you might consider some sort of exercise at home. At present there is some confusion as to what kind of strength training is most beneficial for rock climbing. Generally speaking, effective training develops certain parts of the body in order to improve a specific performance; but rock climbing calls upon diverse mental and physical skills. Obviously the more training resembles climbing movement the more beneficial it will be. Pull-ups, for instance, will be of far more value than press-ups. In fact, the pull-up exercise has been commercially exploited by companies

Fig 17   The Bendcrete indoor climbing wall at Kelsey Kerridge Sports Hall, Cambridge.

producing bolt-on training aids for use at home (presumably because door lintels lack sufficient strength or sophistication for today's climber).

As a general rule, strength training seeks to develop the muscle fibres by prolonged working of the muscle near – but not at – its maximum capability. Bearing this in mind, pull-ups may tax undeveloped muscles so severely that the exercise cannot be sustained. Partial foot support will reduce the load (and the likelihood of injury) but increase the period you are able to exercise. Some climbers develop arm strength, stamina and dynamic attitude by speed climbing without foot support up gymnasium ropes or the underside of rung-and-rope ladders. Effective though this is, it places great strain on untrained arms and shoulders with a severe risk of injury.

Some types of training are less directly beneficial but are useful for improving general fitness and flexibility as well as creating a sense of overall well-being. These include yoga, stretching exercises and running. Coupled with these you might also consider adopting a suitable diet to help attain, or maintain, an optimum body weight. Savage weight-reducing diets, however, will diminish your ability to cope with climbing on large or remote cliffs.

There is no doubt that training and exercise will help you realise your potential, but unless you have an ambition to rise to the forefront of technical achievement there is no *need* to adopt formal training at all. Besides, the most enjoyable way to train for climbing is to climb.

5 Hard Rock

'There are only two grades of climb', I was once told, 'those you can get up and those you can't.' A simplistic view perhaps, but one that helps to explain why one person may retreat baffled from a *Diff* while another glides effortlessly up an *Extreme*. The point is that somewhere along the rising scale of difficulty you will begin to encounter problems which make special demands on your abilities. Precisely where these will begin depends on your physique and psyche, as well as on the peculiarities of the grading system, but encounter them you will.

In clinical terms the differences between neighbouring *VDiff* and *VS* routes (or for that matter between *VS* and *Extreme* routes) simply amount to their steepness, continuity, and size or spacing of holds. In real terms those differences make quite separate demands on your strength, stamina, technical ability, motivation, commitment, self-control and equipment. It is the same game but played in a different league.

The historical precedents for seeking out hard rock climbs were established during the earliest days – such was the nature of rock climbing and the character of the people who migrated to it from hill walking. Standards of difficulty in the sport have continued to rise ever since, pioneered by its innovators and consolidated by its mainstream. This upward trend, however, is much less significant than your own progress through the grades. The actual letters and numbers are in themselves unimportant; what matters is daring to enter a new realm of contest.

COMPONENT PARTS

Writers like to explore the mind game of hard climbing but risk alienating readers who may be unfamiliar with the ground rules or terminology. I have resisted the temptation to follow that road, but will try to isolate and analyse – not too deeply – the component parts of hard climbing. The risk now is in upsetting those who like to preserve the mystique of hard rock. I think it can be justified; despite what you may hear to the contrary, the majority of 'hard' climbers adopt a structured approach to their routes. There is certainly scope for inspired climbing, but even that builds on a clinical preparation.

Inspiration

The inspiration to attempt a hard climb may come from one of several sources. Guidebooks recognise classic status and indicate quality using a star system, but the modern style of writing is so condensed that there is no longer room for elaboration. Conversely, lavishly illustrated route compilations, such as *Hard Rock* and *Extreme Rock*, have space fully to indulge their readers with palm-moistening action photographs and persuasive rhetoric. In fact, such books inspire some climbers to pursue the list of routes with the zeal of train-spotters –

puerile but fun.

Guidebook writers too easily underestimate the efficiency of word-of-mouth communication within the climbing community. A single enthusiastic climber propped strategically against a crowded bar on a Saturday night can do more for the popularity of a hard new route than any amount of edited eulogising in a *New Routes* supplement to the guide. By these means a modern classic may receive a hundred ascents before the revised guidebook reaches print.

For all that, the most lasting source of inspiration is the rock itself. It could be that an impressive rock feature once caught your eye, or the sight of climbers at work on a test-piece planted the seed of emulation.

Motivation

Inspiration lies dormant until ignited by curiosity. At first it may be the lure of personal status which motivates you to attempt routes of reputation. Inevitably this mellows with time until the combination of personal challenge, climbing quality, and the prospect of exciting situations becomes inducement enough.

Information

Once attracted by a route, the next step is to find out whether or not your advances are likely to be welcomed or rebuffed. You will know from the route grades whether or not the climb is feasible, but that is not the whole story. For instance, you will want to know the nature of the main difficulties and their proximity to protection. It could be that you are prepared to attempt a well protected crack graded E2 5c, but not a poorly protected slab at E1 5b. Sometimes the guidebook description omits even this basic information, so it helps if you can speak to someone who has already done the climb. A throw-away comment like 'protection is good where it matters' or 'not as sustained as Left Wall' (or some other climb you know well) can be worth half a page of written information.

Physical and Mental Preparation

Generally speaking, it is unrealistic to train for a specific route, although you may need to postpone the attempt to allow for some training if bad weather or illness has kept you off the rocks for a few weeks. Don't be fooled by pub bravado, however. More often than not the heavy drinkers and late night revellers are the ones you will see lowering off their routes the next day. It might sound prim to suggest saving the booze for the celebration, but you can't have it both ways. A hard route is challenging enough as it is, without having to cope with throwing up your breakfast on the stance.

I doubt that any two climbers mentally prepare for a hard climb in the same way. I myself try to visualise the crucial moves, purposely imagining them to be steeper and more difficult than they can possibly be. This leaves me hopping with nervous anxiety by the time I reach the foot of the climb, but because the reality is much less intimidating than the dream I soon relax and start to enjoy the relatively modest difficulties of the climb – or so the theory goes!

Fig 18   Memory Lane (E3), Dinas Cromlech.

Climbs and Climbers

Choice of Companions

The harder the climb, the greater the significance of the lead – but the partnership aspect is no less important than on easier routes. Obviously you will be looking for moral support from your partners when the going gets tough, but – hard climbs being what they are – you had also better make sure they (and you) know how to stop plummeting bodies.

The partnership works both ways. Your responsibility as leader is to do your best to ensure that your companion also enjoys the day. Sadly, some climbers are happy to co-opt inexperienced seconds as portable belays for their attempts on hard routes, knowing full well they have little hope of following the pitch without liberal assistance from the rope. Ideally you should try to find someone of comparable ability with whom to share the leads and the adventure. If his or her climbing skills and predilections happen to complement your own, so much the better.

Special Equipment

The second section covers basic equipment; here we shall just look at special equipment for hard rock. Effective footwear is no less important than strong fingers. High-friction rubber helps, although the actual make of boot is not crucial – despite what the advertisements say. It is more important that uppers fit snugly and soles flex to suit your preferred style of climbing. In general, the lateral stiffness of edging boots suits precise footwork and small holds, whereas the flexibility of smearing boots suits friction moves and sloping holds. Your eventual choice is a compromise, of course, but the aim is to feel confident in what you wear.

You need only experience a hard work-out on a climbing wall to appreciate the advantages of chalk. Firstly it dries the sweat from fingertips and palms to improve grip on everything from pinches to jams. Secondly, the ritual act of dipping your fingers before a hard move mentally prepares you for the task ahead – the self-help equivalent of silent prayer. Improvement in grip is less evident outdoors, but worth having none the less. Valid objections to chalk linger on (the search for an environmentally acceptable alternative continues), and it is undoubtedly true that the greatest benefits are felt by those attempting high grade climbs, but the suggestion that only those climbing above a certain standard *deserve* to use it does not warrant discussion.

Restrictive clothing severely hampers acrobatic climbing movements and yet it often happens that fashion not function dictates what we wear. Happily the two coincide at present in stretch tights, tracksuit trousers, and so on.

The law of self-preservation states that the more exacting the climb, the more protection you will want to place. Apart from an overall increase in quantity you may also choose to augment your standard rack with micro-wires (for protecting a hard move when nothing else will fit), and sprung camming devices (for the rapid protection of strenuous jamming or roof cracks). At the same time you might try to achieve some consistency in your racking system so that you can quickly select the correct nut without having to sift through the whole assortment. Hopefully your enquiries about the route

Fig 19 The Snake (E2), Craig y Forwyn.

will reveal which size of nut will be most useful and which you can safely leave behind. The more weight you can save by these means the better.

Timing and Conditions

Some skill is required in choosing routes which are unaffected by the prevailing weather. Adverse conditions affect all types of route, but if you are climbing at your technical limit you will have nothing in reserve for dealing with poor friction or cold fingers. Even a slight amount of drainage at the rear of a crack can foil an attempt.

A classic route may attract the attention of several parties over a weekend and delays could amount to two hours or more. Moreover, it can be an unnerving experience having to watch someone struggle on your proposed route as you wait your turn below – especially if they fall off! The answer is to start early or choose a quieter midweek day for your attempt.

Sea cliffs are subject to additional variables which limit the choice of route. These include wind strength (big waves), state of the tide, and seasonal restrictions on climbing imposed for the protection of nesting birds. Tide-tables cost just a few pence from stationers and chandlers in coastal areas, whereas provisional dates of seasonal restrictions are usually indicated in the guidebook and confirmed on notices posted near the cliff tops.

Execution

This is it. With considerable effort and determination you have got yourself to the right place at the right time with the right person. All you have to do now is climb the route!

The greatest danger at this point is in ruining your chances by tensing up. The line between being 'psyched up' and being hopelessly 'psyched out' is a very fine one. Think of it this way: you have at your disposal various finite resources – strength, stamina, runners. With your infinite skill and wisdom you will see to it that none are exhausted before the pitch is finished. Does all this sound too cool and calculating? Don't worry, in practice your head will buzz with so many weird sensations that you will be glad of that nagging inner voice which tells you when to rest, place protection and make commitments.

Most hard climbs consist of difficult sequences strung between larger holds where you can rest and place protection. The most common cause of unexpected failure on hard climbs is lack of confidence; in other words an unwillingness to commit to climbing four or five metres without protection. Stopping in mid-sequence to fiddle with runners is self-defeating because it rapidly drains strength. Consequently you become more nervous, want more protection and lose yet more strength trying to place it – a vicious circle. Eventually the ascent loses all momentum and grinds to a halt in a web of runners. Some routes are so poorly protected that they will be climbed confidently or not at all. The potential rewards here – like the potential falls – are immense.

Falls are inevitable when you are pushing close to your technical limit. Nowadays they have become an accepted part of hard climbing, but that does not mean falling is safe. During the climb, that side of your brain which deals with ropework must continually assess the consequences of a fall so that it can arrange protection according to physics and not wishful thinking. The third section elaborates on this.

A flawed ascent gives far less pleasure than a pure one. The criteria for disappointment are not related to the reaction of others but to your own feelings about the climb. However, most climbers agree that repeatedly lowering off a pitch, resting on the rope, or pulling up on slings constitutes a flawed ascent (indicating that either the route is too hard or there is a lack of commitment). The odd thing about this is that you might return the following weekend feeling no stronger but 'thinking positive' and cruise the pitch.

If a lesson is to be learned from all this it is that hard climbs are solved by first splitting the whole problem into its constituent parts. This way you can devote your attention to each in turn with some chance of cumulative success. Otherwise the task may appear so daunting that you are unable to bring yourself to leave the ground.

EQUIPMENT

Fig 20 Digitation, *a test piece at Brownstone's Quarry.*

6 Personal Equipment

There is little point buying expensive equipment *before* you try rock climbing for the first time. The leader will provide ropes and other technical equipment, and may be able to lend you a helmet and harness. Casual clothing and sports footwear should be adequate for the simple, accessible climbs you are likely to attempt on your first day. If your interest in the outdoors began with hill walking much of your present equipment – boots, functional clothing, emergency items – can also be used for mountain rock climbs. Nevertheless, once you have begun to climb regularly – albeit as a 'second' – your chances of finding climbing partners will greatly improve if you can demonstrate self-sufficiency in personal safety equipment; that means buying rock boots, harness, helmet and belay brake.

FOOTWEAR

Unfortunately the characteristics of walking boots and climbing boots differ in several respects. As a result you may need to buy a pair of each.

Approach Boots

Most valley crags and outcrops can be approached in sports shoes, but only the treaded soles and water-resistant uppers of walking boots are really at home on the screes, bogs and muddy paths leading to remote mountain crags. Lightweight hill walking boots make ideal approach footwear and give adequate support on the easier mountain rock climbs.

Rock Boots *(Fig 21)*

The small footholds typical of harder climbs soon expose the limitations of sports or hill walking footwear. Only rock boots possess the desired combination of qualities which include snug fit, friction sole, longitudinal flexibility and lateral stiffness. Each make will emphasise a particular set of attributes, so your choice of boot should also take into account your preferred style of climbing.

Snug Fit

A snug fit need not imply discomfort. Your rock boot size will usually be one full continental size smaller than you would wear in walking boots (but expect variations in sizing between makes). Rock boots sold in half continental sizes offer the best chance of a good fit. Correct length is of paramount importance. When standing, your toes should just touch the front of the boot (but without curling under). This assumes that toenails have been cut short and you are wearing socks of medium thickness. If you opt for a tighter fit then you may suffer badly on hot days.

Snug width fit depends as much on the efficiency of the lacing as on the shape of the boot. Check that when pulled tight the lace-holes are not drawn too closely

Personal Equipment

Fig 21 Typical smooth soled rock boots.

together, otherwise you will run out of adjustment once socks and uppers have bedded down during use. Unlined suede uppers tend to stretch with use whereas lined or synthetic uppers generally retain their shape.

Sole Friction

Sole friction is difficult to assess because its contribution to overall performance, although significant, dominates only on routes in the higher grades. Most rock boots now use butyl rubber soles. These give more friction than the older carbon rubber type but wear out sooner. Re-soles cost approximately one-third of the price of new boots.

Flexibility

All smooth soled rock boots are longitudinally flexible to ensure maximum friction from the rock in the absence of positive footholds. The degree of lateral rigidity is more variable. *Smearing* boots (flexible) and *edging* boots (stiff) represent the two extremes. Smearing boots are particularly suited to the dynamic approach demanded by gritstone and other types of well-weathered rock, whereas edging boots respond better to the precise footwork demanded by limestone and most types of volcanic rock. A boot which compromises the two properties is probably the best choice.

Mountaineering Boots

Lightweight walking boots lack support on any but the simplest of mountain rock routes. Conversely, plastic double boots commonly used for Alpine or winter climbing are clumsy for walking and lack sensitivity on sloping holds. A good compromise is a *kletterschuhe* – a stiffened medium-weight rock boot fitted with a treaded sole.

CLOTHING

Clothes used for rock climbing are little different from those used for hill walking, except that freedom of movement now assumes the highest priority.

Legwear

Jeans or other non-stretch trousers will do for first climbs but are not satisfactory in the long term. Requirements are a

43

Equipment

close fit (no voluminous folds to obscure footholds) and extreme flexibility (for unrestricted leg movements); both are met in stretch fabrics used in tracksuit trousers (not the baggy type), lightweight climbing breeches and purpose-made climbing tights.

Midwear

Pile fabric – warm, durable and quick-drying – retains its popularity despite a comparative lack of stretch. However, football shirts and sweatshirts have more stretch and are cooler for summer use.

Windproof

Unless the midwear layer is itself windproof (which is unlikely) you will occasionally need additional weather protection. A mountain jacket traditionally fulfils this role, but its pockets, zip and hood will impede movement on all but the simplest of climbs. A simple windproof smock in polycotton or similar material makes a better choice. Since this is unlikely to be made from a stretch fabric you will require a reasonably loose fit. A windproof of this type may also be used without the midwear layer in warm weather.

PERSONAL SAFETY EQUIPMENT

Included in this category are certain specialised items which you will need to buy once you have begun to climb regularly.

Harness *(Fig 22)*

A full body harness or combined chest and sit-harness provides the best support, not only by distributing the load during a fall but also by ensuring that the body does not jack-knife or come to rest in an upside-down position. Both systems tend to restrict movement, however, and almost all British climbers prefer to use the simpler sit-harness. Nevertheless, it is as well to be aware of the shortcomings of a sit-harness, particularly on routes (often the easier ones) where a leader fall could be unpredictable, prolonged or punishing.

Most sit-harnesses conform to a standard design of padded waistbelt plus leg loops. Some leg loops are detachable so you can choose a belt/loop combination to suit your physique. Others are adjustable for girth, which is particularly useful

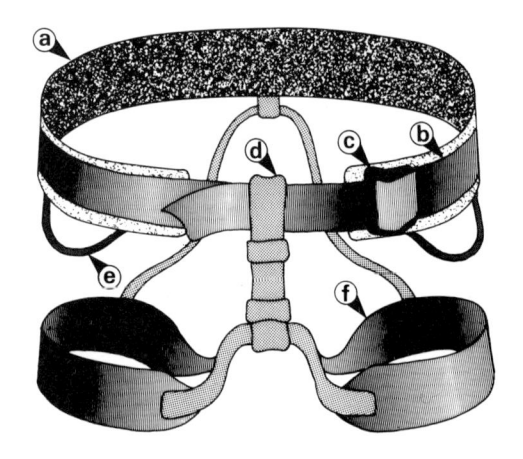

Fig 22 Main features of a sit-harness: (a) waist padding; (b) waist belt; (c) main buckle; (d) rope tie-in loop; (e) gear carrying loops; (f) leg loops.

Personal Equipment

if the harness is to be worn for winter or Alpine climbing.

When buying a harness it is essential to obtain a correct and comfortable fit. Some are more size tolerant than others; this is something you will need to assess in the equipment shop. Comfort comparisons are best made by hanging from each in turn. A good shop will make provision for this. At the same time you can compare the convenience of gear loops and other fittings.

Make sure the harness you buy is sold with written instructions describing precisely how to fasten the buckles and how to tie on to the main rope.

Belay Brake *(Fig 23)*

This is the device through which the main rope is belayed. It consists of an aluminium alloy disc cut by one or, more usually, two slots. Correctly applied, it will exert a braking force on the rope and help you to arrest your partner's fall.

The brake is used in conjunction with a locking karabiner which you will need to buy at the same time. You will also need a length of accessory cord of 4 or 5mm diameter. This cord links brake and karabiner, retaining the brake in its optimum position for smooth rope handling. This position is approximately 10cm from the locking karabiner.

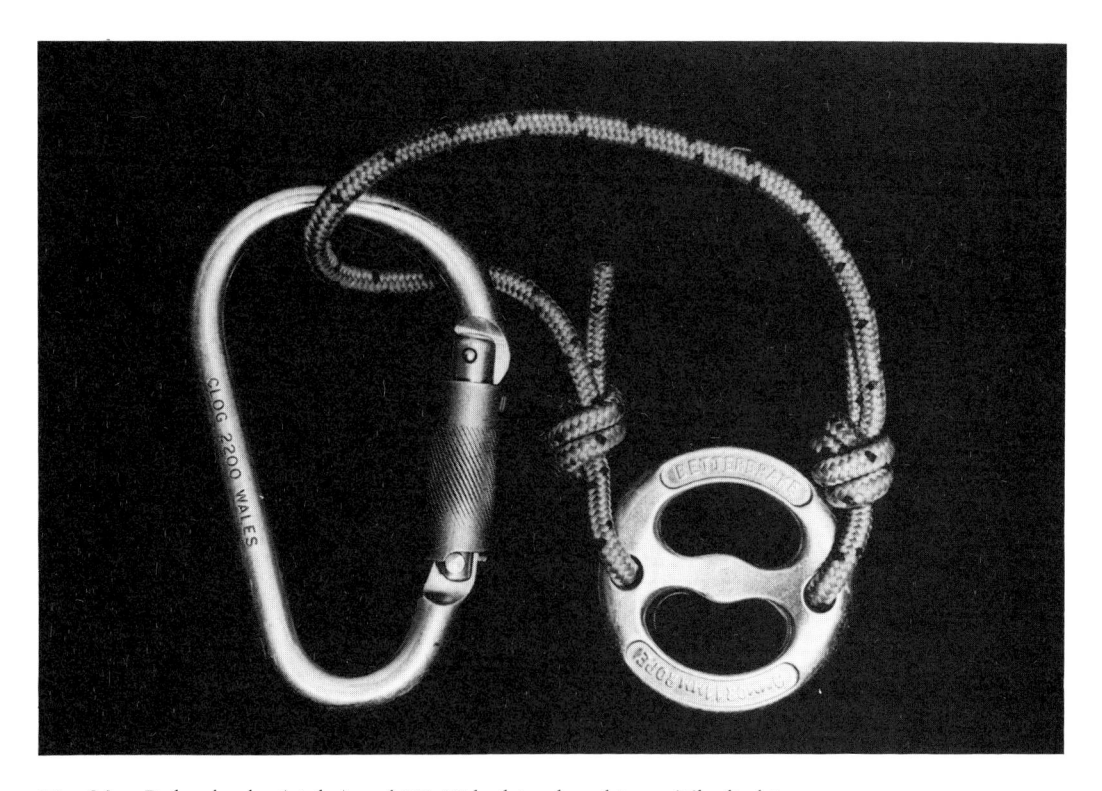

Fig 23   Belay brake (right) and HMS locking karabiner. The linking cord is usually bought separately.

Equipment

Nut Key *(Fig 24)*

This inexpensive device assists with removal of jammed nut runners and helps when threading tape through narrow holes. A typical commercially made key consists of a rigid 20cm metal strip formed into a hook at one end. Some keys also include a facility for aiding withdrawal of camming devices, which are notorious for getting themselves stuck. You might try making your own key from a tent peg or wire coat-hanger.

Prusik Loops

These loops of 6mm accessory cord in 1m and 1.5m lengths (but allow extra for the knots) are invaluable in an emergency. Chapter 11 has the gruesome details.

Helmet *(Fig 25)*

A climbing helmet will minimise head injuries sustained as a result of impact with the rock during a fall or from falling stones. Many rock climbers object to wearing them, partly because of the inconvenience and partly because of fashion. Not surprisingly, beginners tend to be influenced by those currently pushing the technical standards of the sport – very few of whom wear helmets. This is sad because, ironically, those climbing on easier angled cliffs are most at risk from loose blocks and the prospect of a long, tumbling fall.

A full weight helmet gives most protection, but a lightweight version is better than no helmet at all. That said, it is wise to choose one which displays the symbol of UIAA approval. This demonstrates that the design meets certain criteria for strength and resilience. Before buying a helmet check that the dome will not easily push backwards to expose the vulnerable upper forehead.

MOUNTAINEERING EQUIPMENT

Climbing on high or remote mountain crags calls for a certain amount of emergency back-up equipment, although weight must be kept within reasonable limits – especially if the climbing is likely to be difficult. Your decision on what to carry will take account of such variables as time of year, weather forecast, length and difficulty of route, starting time, remoteness and so on.

Food and Drink

Easily consumed items such as chocolate, nuts and dried fruit make excellent hill food. Water or fruit juice is more refreshing than a fizzy drink, and a screw-top metal bottle a more reliable container for it than the cheap plastic variety, which invariably split.

First-aid Kit

First aid for rock climbing performs one of three functions depending on the severity of the injury: stabilising the condition of a seriously injured climber until expert help arrives; re-establishing mobility (especially important on a remote cliff); or simply easing discomfort from minor ailments. The first-aid kit should reflect each of these functions. Here is a suggested list of contents (a plastic lunch box makes an ideal

Personal Equipment

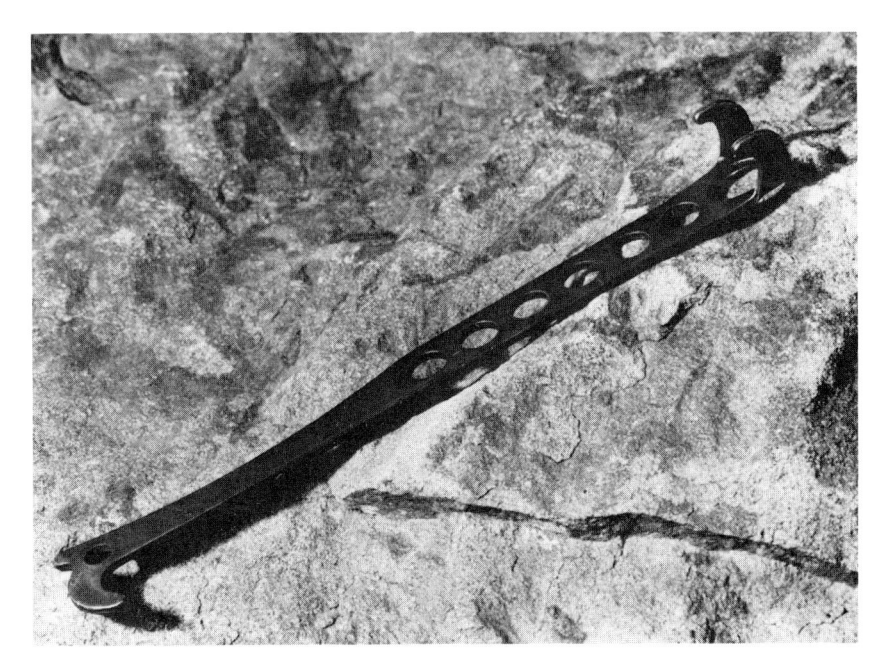

Fig 24   Nut key. The twin hooks are used when extracting Friends.

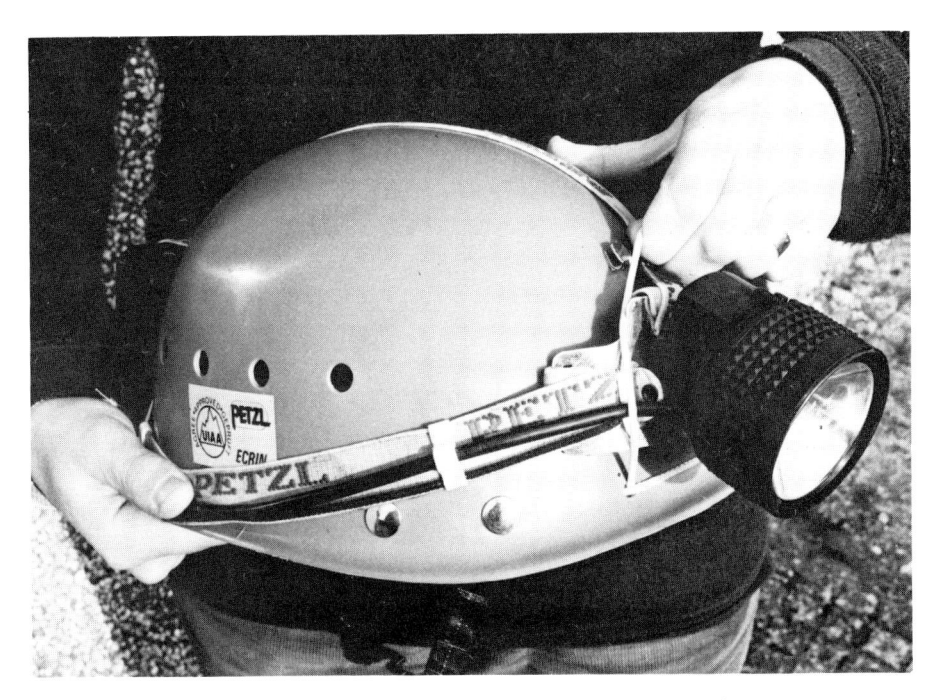

Fig 25   UIAA approved helmet with fittings to secure a headtorch.

Equipment

container):

Small individual plasters
Roll of zinc oxide plaster
Crêpe bandage
Two triangular bandages
Two large wound dressings
Aspirin tablets
Sun cream (when appropriate)
Insect repellent (when appropriate)
Knife (for cutting slings, rope, etc. for improvised splints)
Pencil and paper (for written message of accident location)

Headtorch

Benightment on a big cliff is always a possibility during spring or autumn when daylight hours are few. A headtorch will at least allow you to rig abseils, even if you are unable to finish the climb. At other times it will simply illuminate the return walk from a remote cliff after dusk.

The most reliable torches are those made from a tough plastic and which incorporate a battery housing on the reflector headstrap.

Emergency Bivouac Equipment

It is rarely necessary or practical to carry elaborate bivouac gear. In summer you should be able to survive a night in the open without any special equipment, whereas in spring or autumn a 2.4m × 1.2m (8ft × 4ft) survival bag will protect you and your companion from the worst of the weather. Bags made from heavy-duty polythene are better than lightweight versions in thin polythene or plastic foil (which are unlikely to survive a stormy night, particularly if the ledge is covered in sharp stones).

Spare Clothes

Take what you would expect to carry on a hill walk: woollen hat and gloves, spare pullover, waterproof jacket. Fingerless gloves are useful for climbing on wet or cold rock. During cold weather a thermal Balaclava can be worn underneath a helmet.

Fig 26   Typical 40 litre daysack in heavy-duty nylon. Note the waistbelt for load stability while climbing.

Map and Compass

The guidebook may give explicit instructions for following the climb but will leave you high and dry should you wish to continue to the summit of the mountain. For route finding among rocky terrain the larger scale 1:25,000 maps are superior to those of one-inch-to-one-mile or 1:50,000 scales. A compass will also be required to help with navigation in poor visibility (refer to the bibliography for further reading on navigation).

Rucksack *(Fig 26)*

A rucksack having a slim, uncluttered profile is best when rock climbing (less to jam in chimneys etc.), although a lid pocket will be useful for storing a guidebook and other small items. A rucksack of 25 litre capacity will be adequate for most purposes, but one of 35 or 40 litres would be more useful in winter or for Alpine rock routes. A waist strap tends to foul the sit-harness but greatly improves stability if the climbing is acrobatic.

7 Ropes, Karabiners and Knots

According to popular imagination the purpose of a climbing rope is to drag all members of the party to their deaths – unless, of course, it snaps at an opportune moment and spares the hero. If you prefer to exert some control over your destiny then observe this four point plan:

1. Understand the physical properties of climbing rope.
2. Choose the correct rope for your needs.
3. Take care of your rope.
4. Apply your rope correctly.

Points one to three we can cover immediately; point four will be discussed at length in the third section.

ROPE SCIENCE *(Fig 27)*

The first climbing ropes were made from twisted hemp fibres. These lacked the capacity to absorb energy and would break under the force of a severe fall, unless the belayer had the presence of mind to arrest the fall gradually. The introduction of nylon after the Second World War brought valuable additional elasticity to the hawser-laid construction. Ropes of this type are still made today; relatively cheap and easy to inspect for damage, they have some applications in schools and outdoor centres.

Hawser-laid nylon has since been superseded by ropes of *kernmantel* structure first developed on the Continent during the 1950s. In this construction a softly laid core (*kern*) is surrounded by a protective braided sheath (*mantel*) to produce a flexible rope with excellent handling characteristics.

Continuous nylon fibres are inherently elastic, but up to two-thirds of a rope's total capacity for stretch derives from the way in which the fibres are bound together. It is this enhanced elasticity which allows climbing ropes to absorb fall energy and hence limit the peak force suffered by climber and belay system.

Although energy absorption is by far the most important property of a climbing rope, it must also behave itself when knotted, coiled, gripped, dragged, climbed up or slid down. Within limits a rope designer is able to control such properties as flexibility, resistance to abrasion, gripping and knotting quality, water repellency, strength over sharp edges, and elongation under static body weight.

The UIAA has established a standard to govern the most important properties of kernmantel rope (a British Standard governs hawser-laid ropes). Only those rope types which pass all tests may be awarded the label of approval. The most telling part of the standard is the dynamic test, in which samples of the rope are subjected to a number of severe falls (simulated on a test rig). It is not enough

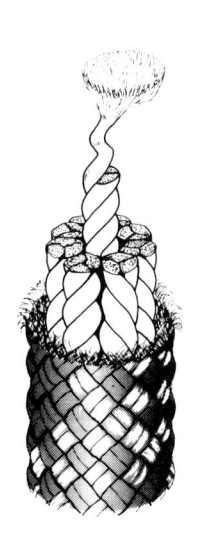

Fig 27   Kernmantel rope construction.

that the samples do not break; they must also demonstrate a capacity to absorb fall energy in a gradual way.

CHOOSING A ROPE

The strength of a rope is closely related to its diameter. The two diameters commonly used in climbing ropes are 9mm and 11mm, although actual diameters may vary by up to 0.5mm from these figures. Ropes of 11mm diameter are used singly, whereas 9mm ropes are used double.

Single rope technique is the easiest to master. Properly applied it is the most convenient method for safeguarding climbs in the lower and middle grades. Despite the possibility of your rapid progression into the higher grades, a single 11mm rope is probably the best initial choice. Later, once the limitations of single rope have become apparent (vulnerability to rope drag, limited abseil capability, etc.), you may decide to switch to double rope technique. However, you only need to buy one 9mm rope as it is standard practice to pair this with a second rope supplied by your climbing partner. If necessary, you could pair the 9mm rope with your original 11mm.

Climbing rope is normally sold in 36m, 45m and 50m lengths. The 36m length is adequate for most outcrop climbing – and is the least expensive – but it will limit you on the multi-pitch climbs of mountain crags. Present guidebooks assume the use of 45m ropes and indicate the location of stances accordingly. Ropes of 50m are less popular in Britain, but that extra 5m can prove extremely useful on long pitches or abseils – particularly on the Continent where 50m ropes are more widely used.

Having made decisions based on length and diameter, and assuming that you will want a rope of kernmantel construction (hawser-laid ropes handle less well and cannot be used with belay brakes), the remaining criteria for choice are less apparent. Rope wears in with use, but you can still get some idea of its handling characteristics when new by forming it into knots, passing it through a belay brake, and performing other standard operations. Suppleness is a much valued property, but not at the expense of a loosely braided sheath which abrades easily and admits damaging grit.

When buying your first rope you are very much at the mercy of the retailer. Provided the rope is of the correct type (single or double) however, and carries the UIAA label, you won't go far wrong.

Equipment

Whatever you do, *never* buy second-hand; every used rope has an unwritten history of misuse.

ROPE CARE *(Figs 28 to 31)*

Nylon climbing rope resists rot but is susceptible to other forms of damage. Careful use and storage will maintain its strength and extend its useful life – and yours too!

Fall Damage

Rope suffers three kinds of traumatic damage during a severe fall: melting, cutting and stress.

The melting temperature of nylon is relatively low and well within that which may be generated when a loaded rope drags across a stationary one. Take extra care when belaying to ensure that the 'live' rope which leads to the climber does not lie over ropes tied to the anchors.

A sharp or abrasive rock edge could cut through a rope during a fall. Guard against this by re-routing the rope away from sharp blocks and narrow cracks.

Nylon fibres are irreversibly stretched when arresting a severe fall. Consequently they lose much of their capacity to absorb energy. Rope replacement is the only cure.

Fig 28   Coiling the rope. Begin by holding a half-metre tail, then add coils formed at full arm stretch.

Fig 29   Note how the coils are allowed to assume a figure-of-eight shape. This helps to reduce kinking.

Fig 30 Turn back the tail and bind it to the coils with the remaining metre or so of rope.

Fig 31 Finally tuck the end through the tail loop and pull the tail to secure.

Equipment

Local Damage and General Deterioration

Falling stones could damage interior fibres while leaving the outer ones unmarked. Rope uncoiled on a ledge is particularly vulnerable. If you suspect damage run the rope slowly between fingertips to check for irregularities.

Embedded grit will cut through interior fibres every time the rope is compressed. Grit can be rinsed out occasionally, but it is still good practice never to stand on the rope.

Outer fibres of the sheath abrade even during normal use. The rope, once smooth and shiny, eventually becomes furry. Although not worrying in itself, this type of superficial damage is indicative of general deterioration.

Care in Transit and Storage

Obviously, climbing ropes must never be used for purposes such as towing or securing luggage to a roof-rack, but there are other, more subtle, precautions to be taken.

Neat coils tend to trap kinks within the rope, so it may be better to allow coils to assume a more natural figure-of-eight shape. Occasionally dragging the rope over grass, or hanging it over a vertical drop, also helps to remove kinks. It has been shown that feeding rope directly into a bag or rucksack – a method used in caving – is the surest way of avoiding kinks and tangles. However, the climber would then face the inconvenience of having to carry a bag up the route solely for this purpose.

Some chemicals attack nylon. Investigations of broken ropes frequently reveal the cause to be contamination by battery acid. Long term exposure to ultraviolet radiation in sunlight can have a similar effect (which explains drastic strength reductions of otherwise undamaged tape and accessory cord found abandoned on the crags). Ordinary glass is no protection against ultraviolet, so ropes displayed in shop windows or stowed on the rear parcel shelves of cars are also at risk.

Accumulated grit may be removed by rinsing the rope in lukewarm water, after which it is hung to dry in loose hanks away from direct heat. A rope is best stored in a dark, well-ventilated place.

Rope Life

All ropes, however well cared for, gradually deteriorate until eventually they arrive at the end of their useful lives. Unfortunately, there are no reliable means of assessing precisely when that is. As a *rough* guide, a rope used for regular weekend climbing (but otherwise undamaged) will be due for replacement after two years. A rope used infrequently and stored carefully should last up to four years, whereas one subjected to heavy use – perhaps including several minor falls – would be retired after one year or less.

ACCESSORY CORD AND TAPE

Kernmantel ropes of diameters less than 9mm have a variety of applications in protection equipment. The most useful of these cords are those of 8mm, 7mm and 6mm diameters; 5mm and 4mm cords are used for secondary applications such as in harness gear loops. Accessory cord is generally sold off-the-reel by the metre.

An important difference between climbing rope and accessory cord is the latter's *static* (low stretch) property. This accounts for the apparent anomaly of an 8mm cord having a higher static breaking strength than a 9mm climbing rope. It follows that long lengths of accessory cord are poor energy absorbers and should not be used in place of a climbing rope – not even as a top rope on small outcrops.

Nylon tape or webbing – being flat and flexible – is especially useful for girdling spikes, threading natural chockstones, and extending runner placements to prevent rope drag. It is sold in widths 10mm to 25mm, in standard or 'super' thickness, and in flat or tubular construction. Standard thickness tubular tape flexes well but knots poorly; thicker tape, though stiffer, resists damage from sharp rock better. Tape can also be bought by the metre, but commercially stitched slings and extenders are stronger and neater (note that the stitching operation is *not* a do-it-yourself task).

Accessory cord and tape are subject to the same kinds of damage and deterioration as the main climbing rope, so preceding advice regarding rope care and replacement apply equally well here.

KARABINERS *(Figs 32 & 33)*

There are two main types of karabiner: *locking* and *ordinary*. Both are made from aluminium alloy bar forged into approximate D-shapes and fitted with sprung gates. The gates of locking karabiners are further secured by a metal sleeve which screws over the latch. On some designs (*Twistlocks, Kwiklocks* etc.) this sleeve is spring-loaded and locks automatically on release.

Locking karabiners are used whenever there is a risk of ordinary gates opening accidentally. Their main applications are in belaying and abseiling.

A karabiner of the self-locking HMS design (pear-shaped) is the most convenient to use with a belay brake or Italian friction hitch. Conveniently large, it promotes smooth running of the rope. HMS karabiners are usually rated 2,200kg (static breaking strength). Locking karabiners used in other situations can be of the cheaper D-shaped screw type (usually rated 2,500kg).

Ordinary karabiners are cheaper, light-

Fig 32 Locking karabiner.

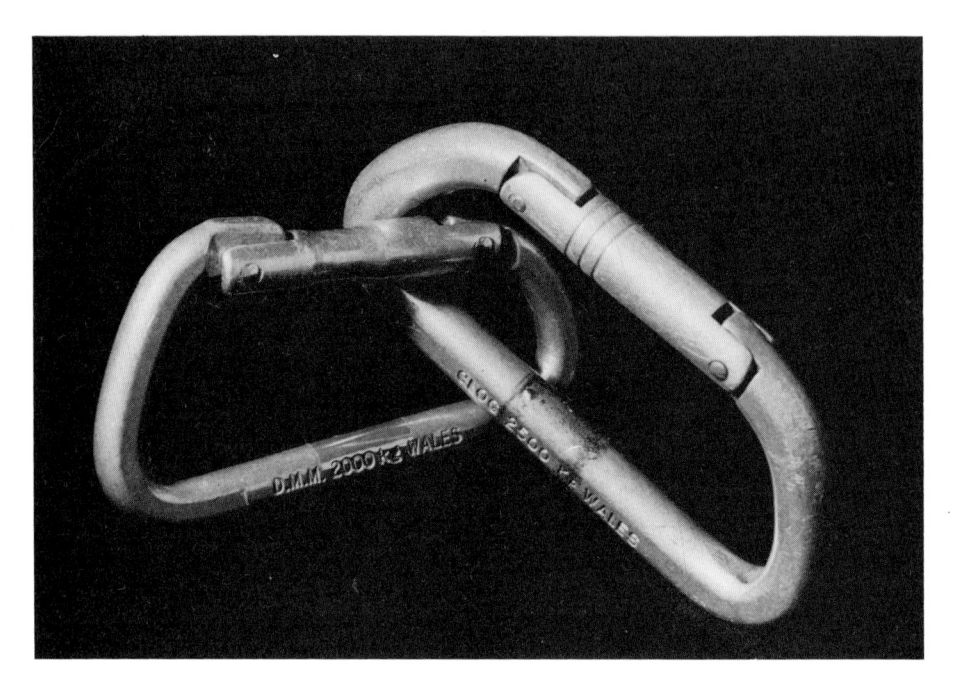

Fig 33 Ordinary (non-locking) karabiners: (left) a 2,000kg lightweight and (right) a 2,500kg standard.

er and quicker to open than locking versions. They are generally used for linking runners to the main climbing rope. The leader may carry twenty or more ordinary karabiners, most of which will be rated at around 2,200kg. A modest weight saving may be made by using lightweight karabiners (rated at around 2,000kg) in conjunction with microwires and other types of flimsy protection.

Although breaking strengths quoted for karabiners far exceed theoretically predicted loads, the safety margin is essential to minimise the risk of failure in unfavourable circumstances. It could happen, for instance, that during a fall the load is brought to bear after the gate has been flicked open by a rock projection or sudden tensioning in the rope. The strength of a karabiner is severely reduced when the gate is open (particularly the lightweight types), and if the load is applied through a broad tape – which further exploits its weakness – it may break. Chapter 10 has some suggestions on how to avoid the improper loading of karabiners.

Sea water and spray corrode aluminium alloy, so after climbing on sea cliffs it is wise to rinse karabiners in fresh water. There is no evidence to support traditional advice to discard alloy karabiners which have been dropped on to a hard surface. It seems this is a hangover from the days of steel karabiners which were vulnerable to internal fracture from this kind of abuse. However, if inspection reveals damage to the gate (such that it fails to close properly by itself) it would be wise to retire the karabiner to a secondary role, such as carrying prusik loops or nut key.

Ropes, Karabiners and Knots

KNOTS

Each of the knots illustrated has several applications. Your decision on which knot to use for a particular application will be based on comparative strength, security and convenience. However, *all* knots weaken the rope to some extent (up to a third) and *all* require checking for tightness. Only essential knots and their main variants (plus a few others of special interest) are given. Some knots may be tied in several different ways, but only the most common are illustrated.

Some knots are secured by a stopper knot. Although this adds nothing to the overall strength of the knot (and in any case frequently comes undone), tying it will at least ensure that you have formed the main knot with a sufficiently long tail.

When buying accessory cord or tape for making up runners you will need to make an allowance for the knot. Assuming that the double-fisherman's will be used for accessory cord and the tape knot for tape, add these approximate lengths to your estimates:

5mm cord – 35cm
6mm cord – 40cm
7mm cord – 45cm
8mm cord – 50cm
15mm tape – 45cm
25mm tape – 55cm

Double Stopper Knot *(Fig 34)*

Main applications Securing the tail of a main knot.
Advantages Less likely to loosen than a simple thumb knot or half hitch (not illustrated).
Disadvantages Consumes more rope than a simple stopper knot.
Special notes Tie the knot very close to the main knot and check frequently for tightness.

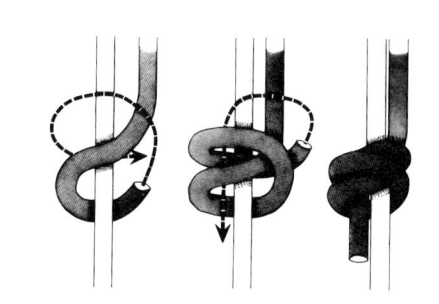

Fig 34 Double stopper knot.

Bowline *(Fig 35)*

Main applications Attaching main rope to harness. Tying direct to main rope in absence of harness.
Advantages Easy to adjust for tightness.
Disadvantages Can work loose (especially in stiff rope).
Special notes Settle the knot carefully when tying to prevent it from distorting into a slip knot. Secure with a stopper knot.

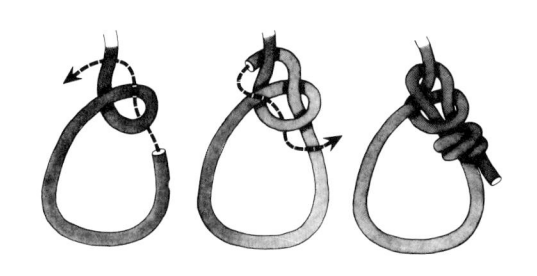

Fig 35 Bowline.

57

Equipment

Figure-of-eight *(Fig 36)*

Main applications Tying direct to main rope in absence of harness. Attaching to middle of rope. Securing to belay anchors.
Advantages Simple to tie. Versatile.
Disadvantages Difficult to adjust for tightness.
Special notes Secure with stopper knot (unless tied in middle of rope).

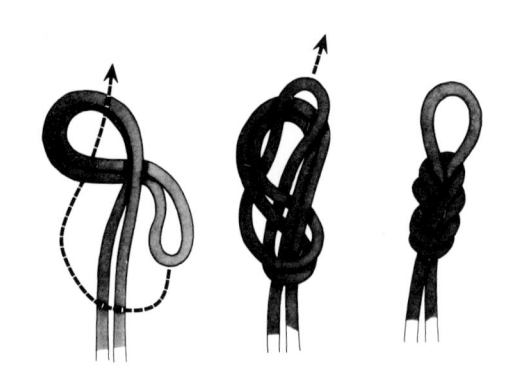

Fig 36 Figure-of-eight.

Threaded Figure-of-eight *(Fig 37)*

Main applications Attaching main rope to harness.
Advantages Less likely to loosen than bowline.
Disadvantages Fiddly to tie. Difficult to adjust for tightness.
Special notes Secure with stopper knot.

Clove Hitch *(Fig 38)*

Main applications Securing to subsidiary belay anchors. Means of attachment to protruding pitons to reduce leverage.
Advantages Simple to tie. Easy to adjust for tightness.
Disadvantages Weakens rope more than figure-of-eight when used for securing to belay anchors.

Fig 37 Threaded figure-of-eight.

Italian Friction Hitch *(Fig 39)*

Main applications Alternative to the belay brake. Direct belaying. Alternative to descender for abseiling.
Advantages Less vulnerable to misuse than the waist belay. Versatile.
Disadvantages Difficult to offer a tight

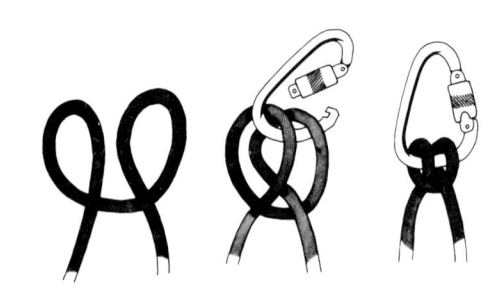

Fig 38 Clove hitch.

rope to the second when belaying. Impractical for belaying double rope.
Special notes Best used in conjunction with an HMS self-locking karabiner.

Double Fisherman's *(Fig 40)*

Main applications Forming loops in accessory cord. Joining two main ropes for long abseils.
Advantages Stronger and more secure than the single fisherman's knot (not illustrated).
Disadvantages Difficult to tie. Consumes more rope than single fisherman's.
Special notes When making up runners: allow sufficient rope for long tails (approximately 8 times the cord diameter). Load with body weight to tighten. Secure tails with plastic tape to minimise tangling. Check frequently for tightness and monitor the gradual 'creep' of tails back into the knot (retie if necessary).

Tape Knot *(Fig 41)*

Main applications Forming loops in tape.
Advantages Only knot suitable for joining tape.
Disadvantages Fiddly to tie. Can work loose easily. Less strong and less neat compared to commercially stitched loops.
Special points Allow sufficient tape for long tails (approximately 5 times the tape width). Load with body weight to tighten. Secure tails with plastic tape to minimise tangling. Check frequently for tightness and monitor the gradual 'creep' of tails back into the knot (retie if necessary).

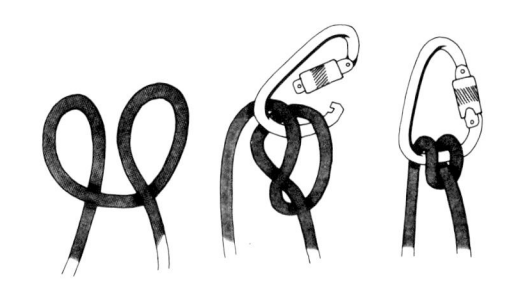

Fig 39 Italian friction hitch.

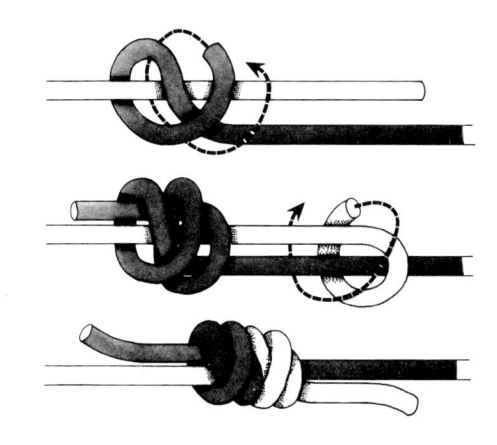

Fig 40 Double fisherman's.

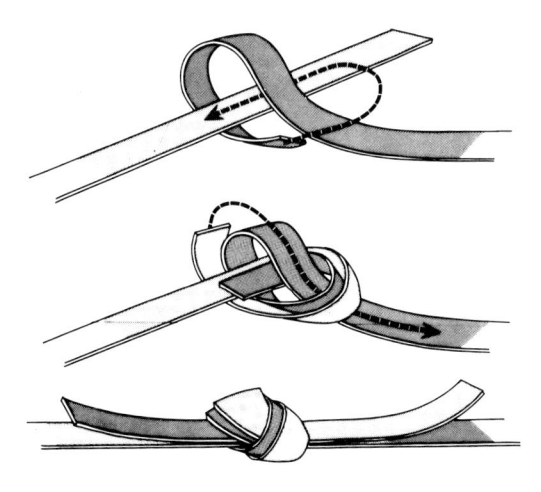

Fig 41 Tape knot.

Equipment

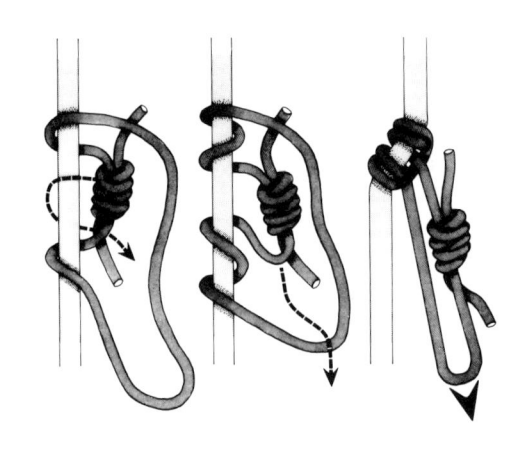

Fig 42   Prusik knot.

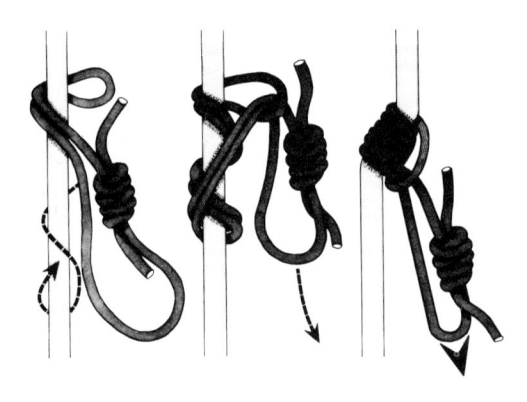

Fig 43   Klemheist knot.

Prusik Knot *(Fig 42)*

Main applications   Temporarily securing the main rope to belay anchors (*see* Chapter 11). Ascending fixed ropes.
Advantages   Simple to tie (one-handed with practice). Light, inexpensive alternative to ascending devices.
Disadvantages   Can be difficult to release after loading. Could fail if subject to shock loading.
Special points   Efficiency depends on relative diameters of rope: 7mm cord works well on 11mm climbing rope, but 5mm is better for 9mm ropes; 6mm cord is a good compromise.

Klemheist Knot *(Fig 43)*

Main applications   Temporarily securing the main rope to belay anchors (*see* Chapter 11). Ascending fixed ropes.
Advantages   Gives variable friction (depending on number of turns). Easier to release after loading than the prusik knot.
Disadvantages   Difficult to tie one-handed. Could fail if subject to shock loading.
Special points   Efficiency depends on relative diameters of rope: 7mm cord works well on 11mm climbing rope, but 5mm is better for 9mm ropes; 6mm cord is a good compromise. (As a last resort it may be formed using a tape loop.)

8 Protection Equipment

This chapter describes protection hardware – slings, nuts, camming devices – and how to place them (pitons are discussed in the aid climbing section of Chapter 12). Chapters 9 to 12 tackle the wider question of how to apply protection to safeguard the climb.

EVOLUTION OF THE NUT

The concept of an intermediate or 'running' belay (hence the term *runner*) is almost as old as the sport itself. A cunning nineteenth-century pioneer would untie from his rope and thread the end behind a stone wedged in a crack before retying to resume the struggle. Thus protected, he might have attempted a gully pitch which otherwise would have been considered unjustifiable. In later years line slings and karabiners substituted for rope threading, while a pocketful of stream pebbles made good the shortage of natural chockstones.

In retrospect the evolution of technical equipment in rock climbing seems exasperatingly slow. It was not until the early 1960s that climbers realised the true potential of artificial chockstones. The earliest type was nothing more than an engineering nut, its threads drilled out to prevent chafing of the line sling on which it was threaded. By the end of the decade these 'nuts' had been superseded by an assortment of drilled alloy wedges and hexagonal bars. The term *nut* remains to remind us of their humble origins.

Wedge design during the 1970s concentrated on refining shape and extending the range of sizes. The smallest nuts, being no thicker than the diameter of the finest accessory cord, were threaded onto swaged wire loops – a trend which soon reached its logical conclusion with the brass *micro-nut*.

In the meantime, the regular hexagon shape had been modified into the versatile *hexentric*, in which irregular faces increased the number of placement possibilities to three. Climbers soon discovered

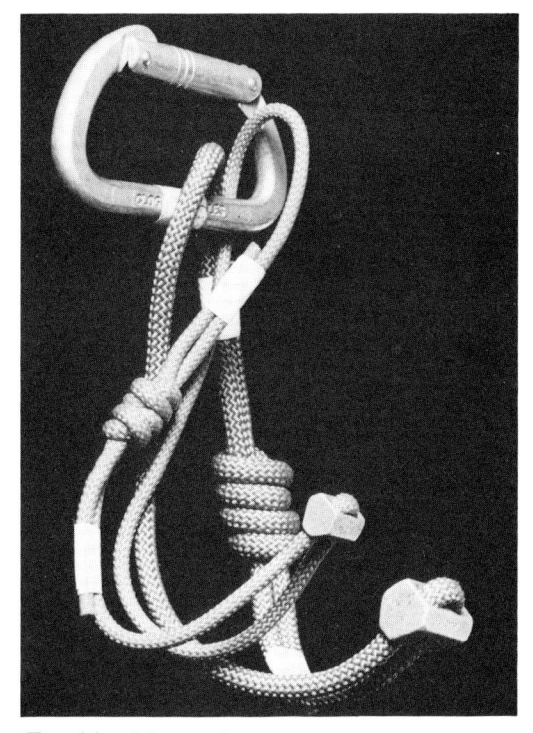

Fig 44   Hexentrics.

Equipment

that the security of two of these positions was greatly enhanced by the twisting or camming action exerted by the cord. Camming nuts proved particularly useful in the normally unprotectable parallel-sided cracks. The *Tri-cam* further explored the camming concept, while the *Friend* – an ungainly gadget bristling with cogs and springs – later exploited the principle to the full. Here at last was the ultimate nut. Not only would it settle into cracks of variable width but – incredibly – would grip in outwardly flaring cracks. Nevertheless, even the smallest Friend will not fit the finer cracks. The pursuit of 'little friends' continues.

Placement Mechanics

Each sling or nut runner reacts only according to the laws of mechanics. If circumstances demand that the runner fails, then fail it will. Blind faith does not enter into it. What you must try to do when placing protection is to suppress anxiety for a moment and adopt a mental state of clinical detachment. Placing protection is not an art but a science.

The maximum load a runner can withstand is limited by its intrinsic strength. In most cases this is the strength of the cord on which the nut is threaded. Medium and large nuts threaded on 8mm cord are potentially as strong as the rest of the rope system, whereas small nuts – which accept only the finer (weaker) wires and cords – are capable of supporting only gentle falls. The nature of the rock dictates what kind of runner you can place. Some routes are notoriously difficult to protect.

The main cause of runner failure is the nut pulling out of its placement, not the sling snapping. Given that most nuts work on a wedge principle, you can improve security by settling the nut just above a constriction (i.e. where the crack begins to widen). That in itself, however, is not enough. The force of a fall has direction as well as magnitude. During a fall the direction of pull on the nut or sling depends on the lie of the rope, the site of the previous runner, and the presence of local obstructions (such as a protruding lip of rock). Seemingly perfect runners will fail if the mechanics of the fall exploit limitations of their placement. Chapter 10 details some of the precautions you can take.

Finally, it could happen that the rock itself defeats your best efforts. Runners are placed at points of weakness; when subjected to the force of a fall it could happen that the flake simply peels off, the crack widens, or the pock hole crumbles. This explains why climbers who have grown old and become wise (or more likely began wise and therefore lived to grow old) never put their complete faith in a single runner or belay anchor and instead seek one or more back-ups.

EQUIPMENT

Long Tape Slings *(Fig 45)*

Type 2.4m tape loops in standard or super thickness, flat or tubular, 15mm to 25mm width, stitched or knotted.
Examples 15mm, 18mm and 25mm Supertape; several makes of standard thickness tape.
Applications Large trees, blocks, natural chockstones. Often used as a belay anchor.

Protection Equipment

Limitations Risk of cutting on sharp edges (especially those of standard thickness) and jamming during removal. Bulky to carry.
Recommendation Two stitched 2.4m × 25mm Supertapes.
Placement Check for sharp edges on blocks and reposition or pad the edge using the knot tails or doubled stitched section.
Precautions Broad tape loads karabiners unfavourably so use with a heavy-duty locking karabiner.

Standard Tape Slings *(Fig 46)*

Type 1.2m tape loops in standard or super thickness, flat or tubular, 15mm to 25mm width, stitched or knotted.
Examples 15mm, 18mm and 25mm Supertape; several makes of standard thickness tape.
Applications Flakes, small spikes, natural chockstones and threads. Also for extending other runners.
Limitations Standard tape is especially vulnerable to cutting on sharp edges. Supertape is better in this respect but may be too thick to place around some flakes and threads.
Recommendation Two or three 1.2m stitched 18mm Supertapes plus one 0.5m knotted 15mm standard tape for constricted placements.
Placement Beware of creaking flakes and rattling spikes. Check for sharp edges and reposition or pad the edge using the knot tails or doubled stitched section.
Precautions Use a longer sling if the angle made by the tape at the karabiner exceeds about 60 degrees.

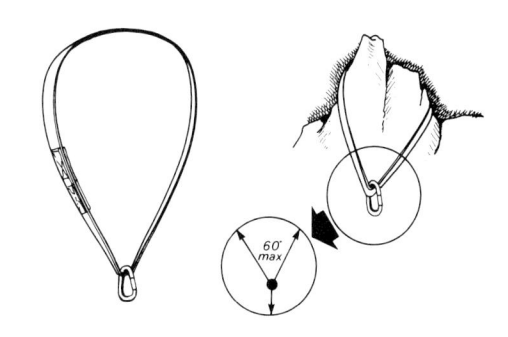

Fig 46 Standard tape slings.

Tape Extenders *(Fig 47)*

Type 10cm to 25cm (doubled length) tape loops in standard or super thickness, flat or tubular, 12mm to 25mm width, stitched or knotted, open loop or stitched, standard or shock absorbing.
Examples Quick-draws, Screamers.
Applications Extending wired nuts to prevent dislodging and to reduce rope drag. Shock absorbing extenders are claimed to protect suspect placements from shock loading.
Limitations Short loops cannot be used for other applications (small flakes and

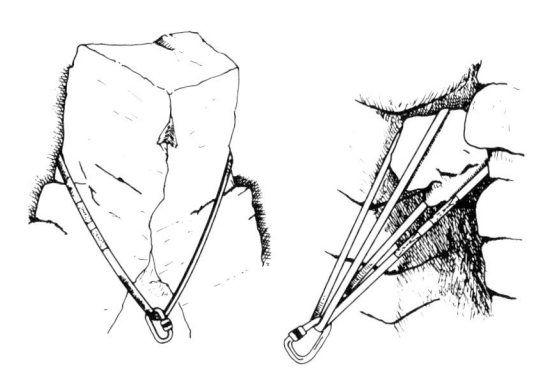

Fig 45 Long tape slings.

Equipment

threads). Broad tape places undue strain on lightweight karabiners.
Recommendation Two or three 12cm × 18mm stitched extenders, plus two 20cm × 15mm stitched Supertape loops.
Placement Used in conjunction with karabiners as a link from wire runner to main rope.
Precautions Never loop directly around wire (great risk of cutting).

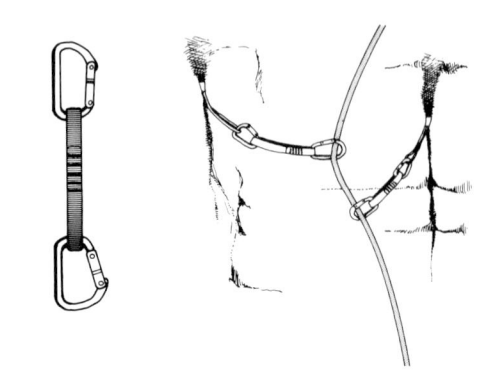

Fig 47 Tape extenders.

Wedges *(Fig 48)*

Type Curved or straight faced aluminium alloy wedges drilled to accept 5mm to 8mm diameter accessory cord.
Examples Rocks, Stoppers.
Applications Widely used for runners and belay anchors in vertical or horizontal cracks, pock holes, pockets, slots, etc.
Limitations Require positive taper for the wedging action to apply. Straight faced wedges are difficult to settle in irregular or crystal choked cracks. Small sizes on 5mm or 6mm cord will not sustain large loads.
Recommendation Graduated range of three or four curved-face wedges on 7mm and 8mm accessory cord.
Placement Look for constrictions in the crack which will prevent outward as well as downward movement. Settle the scooped face around protrusions to minimise swivelling. The wide placement options (i.e. using the two side faces) are generally less stable.
Precautions Cracks behind blocks and spikes may expand under load and release the wedge. Mud or crystals in the crack may give false placements. Beware of sharp edges to the crack over which the sling may lie (especially in horizontal placements).

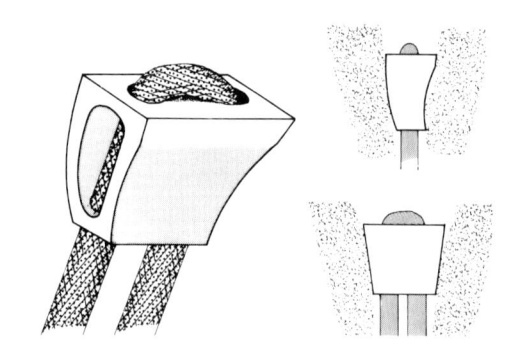

Fig 48 Wedges.

Wired Wedges *(Fig 49)*

Type Curved or straight faced aluminium alloy wedges threaded on 2mm to 4mm diameter wire loops.
Examples Rocks, Stoppers.
Applications As for wedges on cord, but generally used to protect the narrower range of cracks.
Limitations Vulnerable to being swivelled out by normal rope pull. Small sizes are unable to withstand large loads.
Recommendation Graduated range of about six small and medium sized curved face wedges to complement the selection of wedges on cord.

Protection Equipment

Placement As for wedges on cord (plus more possibilities for placing higher or deeper in cracks). Settle with a sharp tug; but be prepared in case it suddenly pulls out!
Precautions Minimise swivelling and rope drag by extending each placement. Carry a nut key to aid removal.

Micro-nuts *(Fig 50)*

Type Straight or scoop faced brass wedges soldered on to 1.5mm to 3mm wire loops.
Examples RPs, HBs, Micro Rocks.
Applications Additional nearby protection for hard moves.
Limitations Low load capability, especially in small size. Require clean and positively tapered cracks. Difficult to remove if placed deep in cracks.
Recommendation Graduated range of three or four (perhaps omitting the smallest and largest sizes) to complement the selection of wired wedges.
Placement As for wired wedges, but it is particularly important to choose and settle the placement carefully.
Precautions Minimise swivelling and rope drag by extending each placement. Check the wire for fraying at its junction with the wedge.

Hexs *(Fig 51)*

Type Irregular hexagon alloy bar drilled to accept 5mm to 8mm diameter accessory cord or 3mm to 4mm wire.
Examples Hexentrics.
Applications Widely used in all types of cracks and pockets (up to fist width) for protection and belay anchors. Particularly useful in horizontal slots. May also be

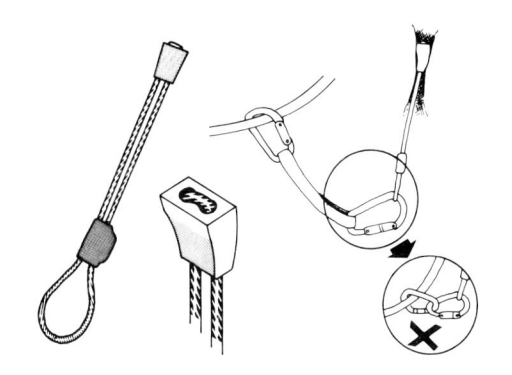

Fig 49   Wired wedges

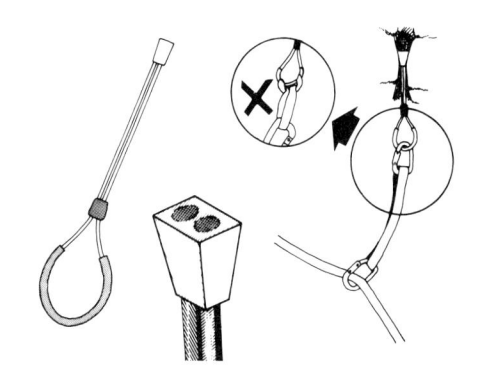

Fig 50   Micro-nuts.

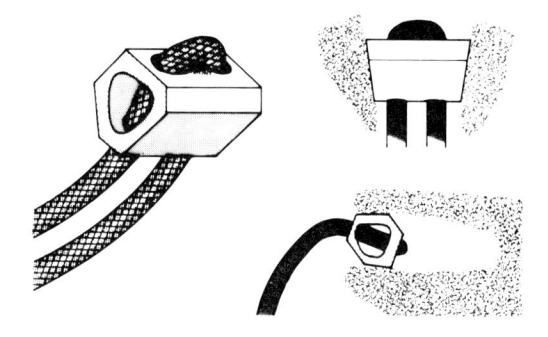

Fig 51   Hexentrics.

Equipment

used to protect parallel-sided cracks.
Limitations Require more considered placement than wedges. Ineffective in very shallow cracks. Small sizes are unable to withstand large loads. Wired versions can be very awkward to place.
Recommendation Graduated range of up to eight Hexentrics on 6mm to 8mm cord (excluding the smallest and several of the larger sizes).
Placement Look first for constrictions or slots which will give a wedge-like placement. In parallel-sided cracks, settle the faces carefully (using one of two width options) and tug the cord to initiate the camming action. The wide (transverse) placement option acts simply as a wedge.
Precautions As for wedges on cord.

Camming Devices *(Fig 52)*

Type Expanding nuts consisting of a spindle fitted with single, double, triple, or quadruple metal cams.
Examples Friends, CAMS, Micromates.
Applications For fast placement when protecting strenuous pitches – jamming cracks, roofs, etc. Also for placement in parallel or outwardly flaring cracks, pockets and slots, and as a weight saving alternative to several large Hexentrics.
Limitations Expensive and heavy unless replacing several Hexentrics. Ineffective in shallow cracks. May be difficult to remove.
Recommendation Graduated range of two or three medium sized Friends.
Placement Try to optimise the placement by settling the cams in a positively tapering part of the crack and using flared placements only as a last resort. Align the stem or wire frame with the probable direction of rope pull during a fall. Avoid placements near the minimum and maximum of the expansion range.
Precautions Take care to minimise leverage on rigid stems in horizontal placements by placing deeper or by tying off with a sling (as for protruding pitons – refer to the aid climbing section of Chapter 12). Carry a nut key which incorporates a facility for aiding removal of Friends.

BUILDING UP A RACK

Buying a full rack of protection gear at the outset will prove costly. Moreover, you will need only a basic selection at first. The following list suggests a means of progressing gradually from a basic to a comprehensive rack. Note that although specific makes and sizes have been mentioned, there are several equally effective alternatives. Note that cord slings fitted to nuts will be about 50 to 60cm long (doubled length). When buying cord remember to make the appropriate allowance for tying the knot.

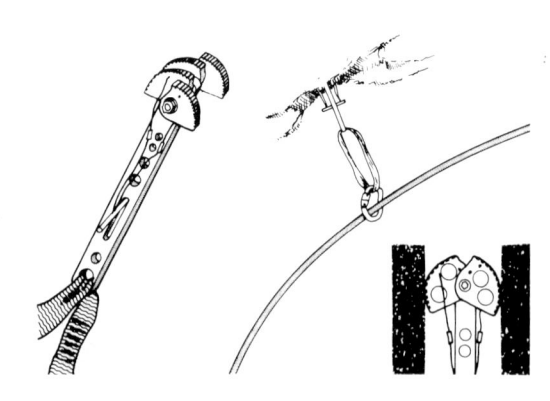

Fig 52 Camming devices.

Protection Equipment

Basic

For first climbs on outcrops, simple multi-pitch mountain rock climbs, etc.

2 × 2.4m/25mm stitched Supertapes
2 × 2,500kg locking karabiners (for above)
2 × 1.2m/18mm stitched Supertapes
2 × 2,500kg ordinary karabiners (for above)
1 × Hex 7 on 8mm cord
1 × Hex 3 on 7mm cord
1 × Rock 9 on 8mm cord
1 × Rock 8 on 8mm cord
1 × Rock 7 on 7mm cord
1 × Rock 4 on wire
1 × Rock 3 on wire
6 × 2,200kg ordinary karabiners (for above)

Intermediate

Multi-pitch climbs of medium difficulty. As above plus:

1 × Friend 3
1 × Hex 6 on 8mm cord
1 × Hex 5 on 8mm cord
1 × Hex 4 on 8mm cord
1 × Hex 2 on 6mm cord
5 × 2,200kg ordinary karabiners (for above)
1 × Rock 6 on wire
1 × Rock 5 on wire
1 × Rock 2 on wire
1 × Rock 1 on wire
1 × 50cm/15mm knotted standard tape
2 × 12cm/18mm stitched extenders
6 × 2,200kg ordinary lightweight karabiners (for above)

Comprehensive

All types of high standard climbs. As above plus:

1 × Friend 2
1 × 2,200kg ordinary karabiner (for above)
1 × RP 4 micro
1 × RP 3 micro
1 × RP 2 micro
1 × RP 1 micro
2 × 10cm/15mm stitched extenders
5 × 2,000kg lightweight ordinary karabiners (for above)

Racking Gear

Protection gear may be racked on a single or twin bandoleer slung over the shoulders (accessible, but gets in the way on low angle rock), or on gear loops fitted to the harness waistbelt (stable, but sometimes awkward to select). Tape slings are generally carried around the neck (easy to remove with either hand but a small risk of strangulation during a fall), or over one shoulder (neater, but cannot be removed by that hand). Long slings are carried double by first twisting into a figure-of-eight shape and clipping the karabiner through both loops thus formed. This prevents loss of the karabiner when the sling is opened out into a single loop.

It is a good idea to rack your runners consistently in some sort of logical order. You will then know precisely what sizes you have and where to find them, even when under pressure on a difficult or strenuous pitch. A typical arrangement would be as follows:

Equipment

Left side (from front to rear) Hexentrics and camming devices (smallest to front).
Right side (from front to rear) Micros on single karabiner; short extenders pre-clipped with two karabiners; wired wedges on single karabiner; long extenders on single karabiner; chain of spare karabiners; wedges (smallest to front).

Rear Belay brake on locking karabiner; prusik loops and nut key on karabiner.

To avoid confusion when pooling equipment with companions it is a good idea to personalise all your runners and karabiners with a band of coloured insulating tape.

TECHNIQUES

Fig 53   The Walk, North Face of Gearr Aonach, Glencoe.

9 Rock and Rock Climbing Technique

In grappling too soon with the technicalities of ropework you risk obscuring the essential nature of rock climbing. Besides, it was probably the thought of clinging to steep walls which attracted you to the sport in the first place, not fiddling with knots and metal clips. Perhaps your first taste came during a hill walk when a grassy shoulder suddenly reared up into a rocky ridge, or while exploring the sea-washed coves of a rugged coastline, or earlier still as a child climbing trees or scaling the wall bars of the gym. Don't let anyone tell you that rock climbing is fundamentally different from any of these experiences – it isn't. What it does do is expand and refine the basic climbing instinct in order to squeeze more sensation from those primitive feelings of daring, fear, balance, effort, achievement and exhilaration. So forget about the technicalities for a while and simply 'think rock'.

ROCK FEATURES

The best place to rediscover and relearn climbing is not on a large cliff but on a fallen boulder or small outcrop. If this is no more than five metres high and has a flat meadow beneath it on which to fall, so much the better.

Unless this boulder is very unusual it will not be smooth and regular like an egg. Instead, one side may overhang while the opposite face lies back as a gentle slab. Perhaps half this slab is covered with narrow ledges, the remainder blank and smooth. The other two walls (assuming this boulder is approximately rectangular) are probably more or less vertical; but whereas one may be pitted with holes like a pumice-stone, the other could be split at intervals by irregular fissures ranging in width from a finger-sized crack to a body-sized slot. Even the junctions between the various faces of the boulder are likely to be dissimilar. The first may be rounded and gently angled; the second sharp like the prow of a ship; the third jutting out in a small roof; the fourth indented by a groove. Each feature is a line of weakness by which you can try to climb the boulder.

Even without knowing anything about climbing you would not attempt to use the same technique to climb the pumice wall as you would, for instance, the wide slot. The texture of the rock and the features which shape it dictate how you must position your feet, curl your fingers and lean your body.

ROCK TYPES

Every move on every climb is unique. The rock climber has a new toy every day. Nevertheless, each rock type has its own characteristic form and texture which will govern the battery of

Fig 54 This arete, with its good but infrequent holds, demands a dynamic approach.

Fig 55 Note how the body shifts to the other side of the arete to make best use of the good right handhold.

Fig 56 By leaning out on this support the feet stay firm on their sloping holds.

Fig 57 Having reached the higher set of handholds, body position reverts to a more natural state with most of the weight taken by the feet.

Fig 58 Corner. The least strenuous method of climbing this smooth corner is by bridging up the opposing walls. Note how the boots are placed flat against the rock for maximum friction.

Fig 59 The left palm pushes against the rock to maintain the bridge while raising the left foot.

Fig 60 The feet could have slipped from their friction holds if the reach for the good handhold had been made sooner than this.

Fig 61 Even though the corner is vertical, it is possible to rest the arms completely before resuming the ascent.

Fig 62 Layback. The start of this crack is too wide for comfortable jamming yet too narrow for wedging. Instead its edge is laybacked to make best use of footholds on the wall to its left.

Fig 63 The body must lean well back to prevent the feet slipping.

Fig 64 The hands are moved alternately up the edge; laybacking is extremely tiring so it must be done quickly and with confidence.

Fig 65 Finally, supported by the positive right foothold, it is possible to pull upright ready to enter the wider part of the crack.

Fig 66 Mantelshelf. Emerging from steep rock on to a flat ledge is not always as easy as it seems, especially when the wall has no positive footholds.

Fig 67 The aim is to attain a body position whereby the weight is supported on straight arms, giving a moment's respite.

Fig 68 When ready, one foot is raised and placed on the ledge – a precarious manoeuvre if the ledge is narrow.

Fig 69 Balance can be restored by reaching up to higher handholds, otherwise the other foot is raised and placed alongside the first.

techniques used to climb it.

Rounded holds and bulging cracks are typical of gritstone and sandstone outcrops. Chimneys, grooves and jutting overhangs – many of them disconcertingly holdless – are other common features. Fortunately the friction provided by these rocks is so good that even blank grooves and slabs may be attempted. The crack climbs demand a broad repertoire of jamming techniques coupled with a dynamic approach.

Quarried grit poses a very different set of problems. Vertical walls sparsely furnished with small, flat holds are typical. Most cracks are ragged, narrow and possibly choked with mud. However, the cracks in popular quarries are usually clean and a delight to climb. Good footwork and strong fingers are your best assets in the quarry.

White limestone is generally less reliable than other rock types, especially where there are lots of holds (cracks, chimneys, corners). The rock encountered on open walls is usually less treacherous. Some varieties of coarse, grey limestone are wonderfully rough and solid. Even so, footholds polished from regular use will be slippery. Most good limestone routes take to the open walls on good (if small) finger holds. Although the climbing is usually less dynamic than on gritstone it can be much more intimidating, calling for composure and strong fingers.

Volcanic rock found in mountain regions varies in character from one area to the next. The climbing on some crags is reminiscent of gritstone; on others, of limestone. In general, volcanic rock shares some characteristics with each.

Other rock types – slate, shale, dolomitic limestone, quartzite and so on – are less common. Each has its peculiarities of form and texture, ranging from the geometric smoothness of slate to the abstract texture of quartzite.

OTHER FACTORS

Loose Rock

Rock suspected of being loose must be climbed in a very calculated way, testing each hold for soundness with a sharp rap of the fist. Jamming and pinch holds are less likely to crumble than protruding block or flake holds. Even so, it is wise to distribute your weight as evenly as possible among the holds. It goes without saying that the lunging techniques so effective on solid gritstone are not appropriate here.

Climbing in Mountain Boots

The type of footwear worn also has a bearing on technique. Whereas rock boots and other flexible footwear are generally placed sideways on small holds, stiff mountain boots are applied more precisely, using the front of the toe while keeping the heel low. Although the technique feels precarious at first, it can prove extremely effective on certain types of rock. The skill of climbing in stiff boots is worth developing if you have Alpine ambitions.

Vegetation

Some crags are cloaked in vegetation. These vertical gardens are full of treacherous weeds which look stout but

Fig 70 Chimney. Broad fissures are climbed by a combination of back-and-foot and bridging techniques.

Fig 71 The pressure bridge is maintained by feet and back, or – when raising the back – by feet and palms.

Fig 72 This chimney soon becomes too wide for back-and-foot and so is climbed by bridging. The technique is similar to that used in bridging up a corner, but is generally more secure.

Fig 73 Eventually the chimney widens too far for comfortable bridging and, with some trepidation, it is quitted for more conventional climbing up one of its walls.

Fig 74 Jamming Crack. Hand-sized cracks can offer excellent, if painful, security. Often the most secure hand jam is achieved by inserting the hand with little finger uppermost and, if the crack allows, bending the thumb across the palm.

Fig 75 Inserting the hand immediately above a narrowing in the crack also improves security and saves strength.

Fig 76 When the foot is securely jammed in this way it is possible to rest the arms for a few seconds.

Fig 77 Where the crack is parallel sided, the toe is inserted sideways and then the ankle twisted upright.

77

Fig 78   An overhang need not be the formidable obstacle it appears, provided it can be overcome quickly.

Fig 79   A bold, confident approach reveals a good handhold above.

Fig 80   Using an undercut hold for the left hand, the long reach is made successfully.

Fig 81   Having made the commitment it is best to complete the sequence before strength starts to fade; an attempt to retreat from this position would almost certainly result in a fall.

which snap like carrots when used as handholds. Trees are normally more trustworthy, but not saplings which are poorly rooted in cupfuls of soil. Bear in mind that most trees on popular climbs eventually wither and die from the decades of abuse, usually accompanying some poor unfortunate to the bottom of the crag.

Damp Rock

Mud-filled cracks ooze slimy water during wet weather and remain greasy for some time afterwards. Water also transforms crumbly lichen into slippery pads. Few routes are untroubled by lichen; those climbed mainly on sloping holds are most affected. In an emergency you can improve friction by pulling wool socks over your boot soles.

Corner cracks are the features most affected by lingering damp; ridges, the least affected. Other factors which influence a crag's drying time include: aspect and altitude, proximity of trees, quantity of drainage from the hillside above, time of year, air temperature, humidity and wind strength. On a windy day in summer, for example, the open walls of a south facing crag at sea-level may dry out from a heavy shower in less than an hour. Conversely, the drainage cracks of a high north facing crag may remain damp throughout the winter months.

CLIMBING TECHNIQUE

In this chapter you might have expected to learn how to climb rock. If so, you will have been disappointed. Elaborate written descriptions of climbing technique bear so little resemblance to the actual experience that they do not deserve the space. Instead you are invited to study the captioned photo sequences and practise some of the techniques depicted when you have an hour to spare at your local crag. Have fun!

10 Rope Technique

Maintaining the rock climbing 'safety net' – the rope and belay system – is a wearying task when you consider that the fall it saves may come only once in a lifetime. However, you can be sure that fate, if it can, will exploit even the tiniest lapse in vigilance.

Most climbers learn rope technique by trial and error, applying it thereafter by force of habit. This leaves far too much to chance. Analysis of the underlying principles of efficient rope technique will reward beginner and expert alike.

For all that, even the best ropework is plagued by uncertainties: misunderstandings, elusive anchors, rope cutting edges. It transpires that the best aids to safety are not elaborate rope methods, but climbing partners who promise not to fall! But when they do – which they will – you had better be ready!

UNDERLYING PRINCIPLES

Communication *(Figs 83 to 90)*

Beginners are reticent when asked to call out 'That's me!', 'Climbing!', and other formal expressions from the climbing vocabulary – especially when their partner is in full view and barely ten metres away. Good rope technique, however, depends on leader and second being aware at all times of the precise status of the other, i.e. whether they are anchored, belaying or climbing. A formal exchange of words (or pre-arranged sequence of rope tugs if verbal communication is impossible) avoids dangerous ambiguities.

Security Overlap

At every stage of the climb both leader and second are in some way attached to the cliff – either by anchors at the belay ledge or by the belayed rope. The principle of overlapped security asks that whenever a changeover takes place – such as when the second arrives at the belay ledge – the means of attachment temporarily overlap. Thus, in this instance the leader will continue to belay the second's rope until the second is safely attached to the anchors.

When actually climbing, this principle is so obviously sensible that it barely warrants mention. Amnesia may creep in at times when the dangers are less explicit – such as when the leader has finished climbing a pitch (but has yet to anchor) or when both climbers have arrived at the top of the climb (but have yet to unrope). Several horrific accidents have occurred as a result.

Belay Anchors *(Fig 82)*

Firm anchors placed at the belay ledge are the prerequisites of effective belaying. That is not the end of it, however. Try to find a ledge which allows you to take up a firm, braced stance; otherwise consider sitting down to improve stability. Remember that the anchors, yourself and

Cyfrwy Arete, Cader Idris.

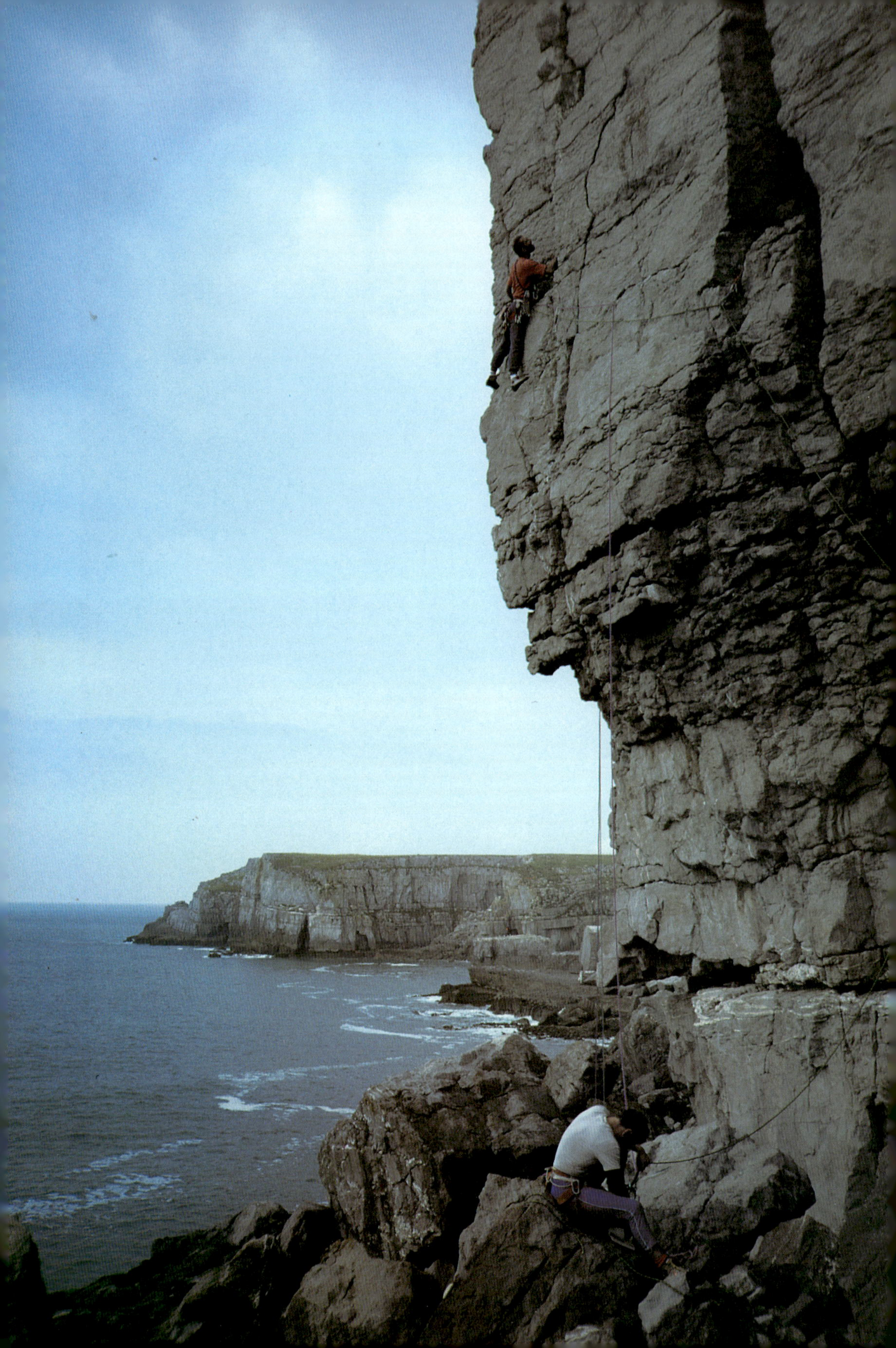

(Left)   Army Dreamers, Pembroke.   *(Above)   An evening bouldering session on Northumberland sandstone.*

Regent Street, Millstone Edge. Many routes in the gritstone quarries were originally climbed during the 1950s using aid; the cleansing effect of a decade of repeated piton insertion (and a fundamental change in attitude) later allowed most to be climbed free.

(Above) Clogwyn du'r Arddu, North Wales. This magnificent cliff holds a special place in British climbing; it has fascinated each new generation of climbers since the first attempts to climb its main buttresses during the 1920s.

(Below) Cadshaw Castle Rock, Lancashire.

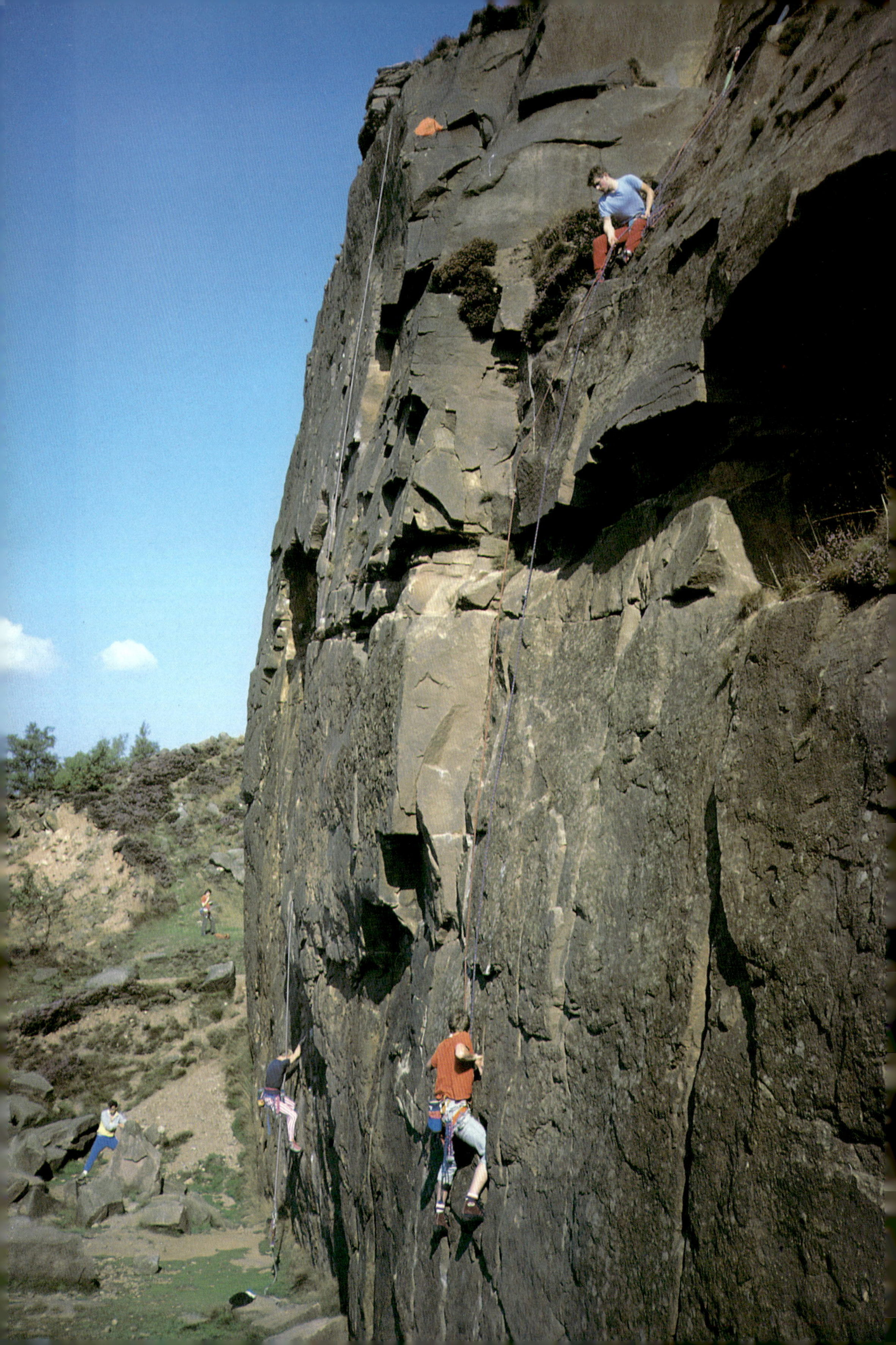

(Left) Gimcrack, Millstone Edge.   *(Above) Great Wall, Clogwyn du'r Arddu.*

Foil (E3), Dinas Cromlech.

Rope Technique

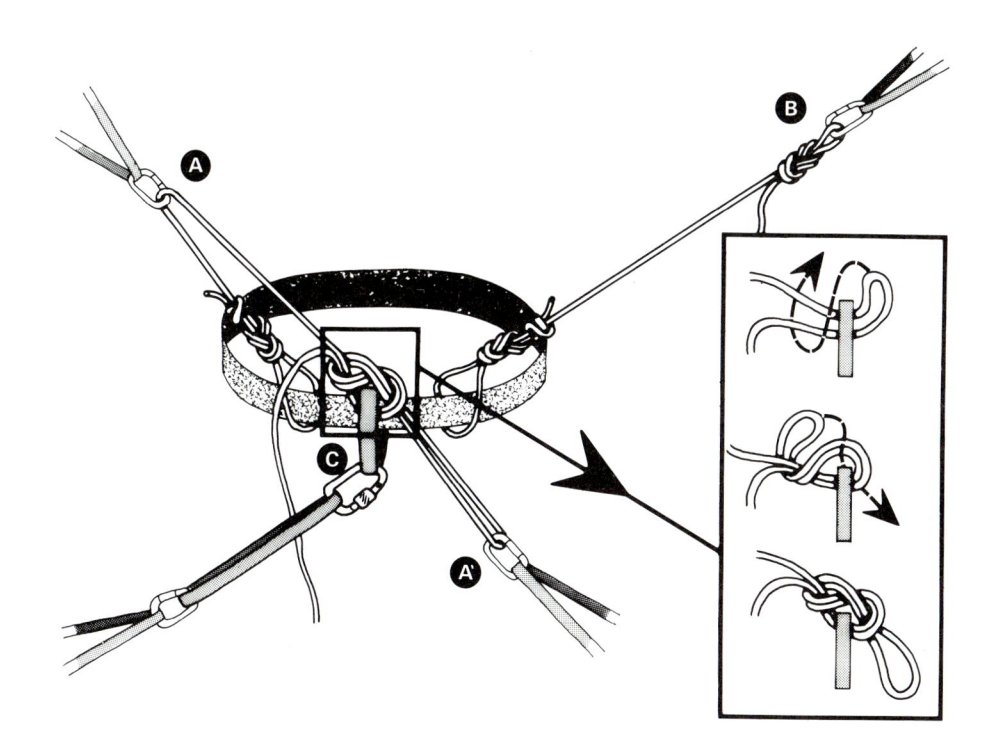

Fig 82 Methods of attaching to belay anchors. (A) Rope clipped through anchor karabiner and tied back to the harness using a modified figure-of-eight knot, which incorporates the harness anchor/belaying loop — see inset. (A') An elongated loop of the figure-of-eight knot may be clipped directly to a second anchor. (B) Figure-of-eight knot clipped into the anchor karabiner. (C) Anchor sling clipped directly to the harness using a locking karabiner. Note that the locking karabiner has been turned gate downwards to prevent the belayed rope from unscrewing the locking sleeve.

the rope together make up a mechanical system. The success of the belay – in other words its effectiveness during a fall – depends on the success of the system as a whole.

There are several different ways of securing to the belay anchors: by clipping a locking karabiner directly between anchor and harness; by knotting the main rope at the anchor karabiner using a figure-of-eight (or clove hitch); or by clipping a loop of the main rope into the anchor karabiner and tying it back to the harness using a figure-of-eight knot.

81

Techniques

Whichever method you decide to use, make sure that when combining belay anchors you can satisfy the following principles:

1. *Load sharing* – so that the stress placed on any one anchor is kept to a minimum.
2. *Independent linking* – so that if one anchor fails, the holding power of others in the system is not jeopardised.
3. *Tolerance to pull direction* – so that the system will resist forces directed from all conceivable directions (such as an upward or sideways pull after the leader has placed protection).
4. *Escape option* – so that if necessary the belayer can secure the fallen climber's rope to the anchors and escape the system (*see* Chapter 11).

Standard Procedure and Communications for Roped Climbing

Fig 83 *The leader climbs the first pitch, placing runners where possible. The second pays out rope through the belay device, ensuring that it runs smoothly even when the leader moves up suddenly. The lower anchor will prevent the second from being pulled upwards if the leader falls.*

Fig 84 *Having reached the ledge at the end of the first pitch, the leader begins to place belay anchors. The second continues to belay the rope.*

Fig 85 *Now secured to the rock, the leader calls down 'Taking in!' On hearing this the second removes the leader's rope from the belay device. The leader now begins to draw up the remaining slack rope. Note that the second remains anchored throughout.*

Fig 86 *When the rope comes tight, the second shouts 'That's me!' The leader belays the second's rope and then calls 'Climb when you're ready!' On hearing this the second begins removing the belay anchors.*

Rope Technique

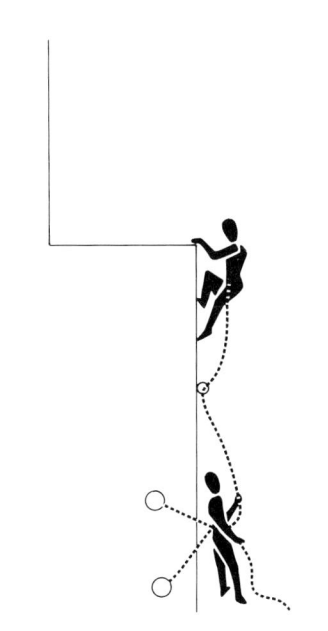

Fig 83

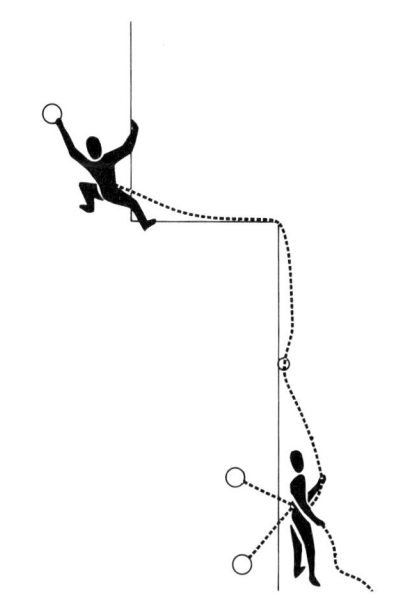

Fig 84

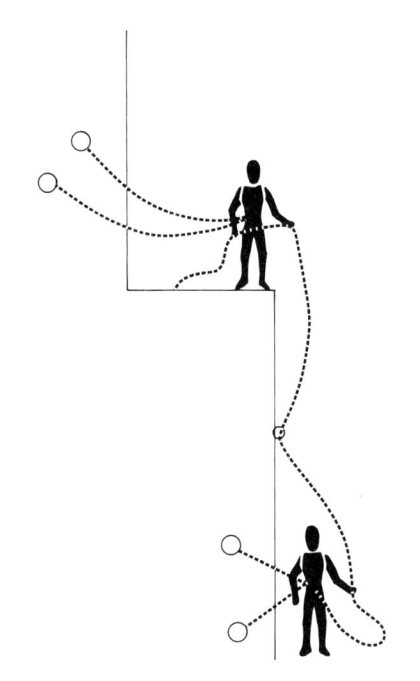

Fig 85

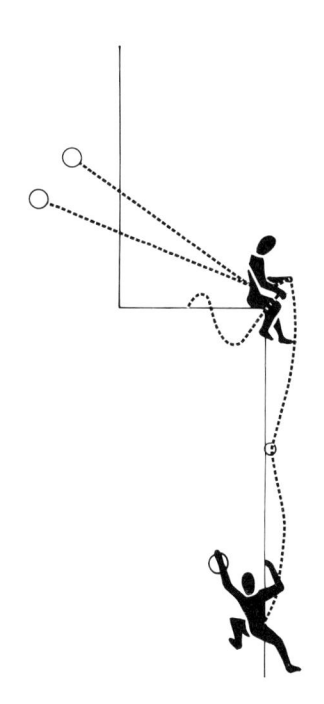

Fig 86

83

Techniques

Fig 87   When ready the second calls 'Climbing!' and ascends the pitch, removing the runners, while the leader draws in rope through the belay device. If too much slack rope accumulates the second calls 'Take in!' If a metre or so of slack rope is required (perhaps while removing a runner) the second calls 'Slack!' If a fall is imminent the second calls 'Tight!'

Fig 88   The second secures to the anchors while the leader continues to belay the second's rope. The second will add a third anchor which will sustain an upward pull.

Fig 89   Now secured, the second belays the leader's rope while the leader detaches from the anchors. Note that throughout this changeover period both leader and second are secured either to anchors or to a belayed rope.

Fig 90   The leader now proceeds to climb the next pitch, placing runners as before to minimise the length of a fall. If a rock is accidentally dislodged the leader calls 'Below!' to warn the second and other climbers.

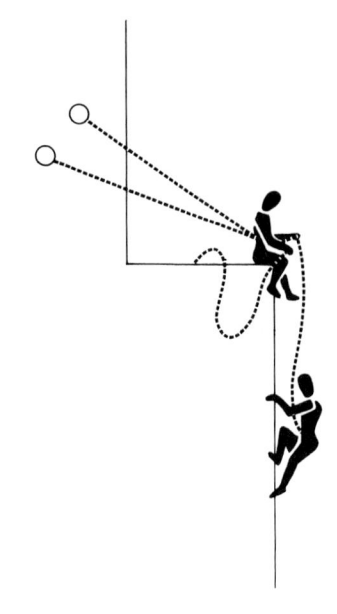

Fig 87

Fig 88

Rope Technique

Belay Methods *(Figs 91 to 93)*

As with anchoring, no single method of belaying the rope is best in every set of circumstances. For this reason it is worth learning a variety *(Figs 91 to 93 detail some methods)*. The waist belay is the most vulnerable to abuse; the Italian friction hitch, the least. All, including the ubiquitous belay brake, depend on proper control by the belayer. It is a fallacy to assume that mechanical belay devices are foolproof.

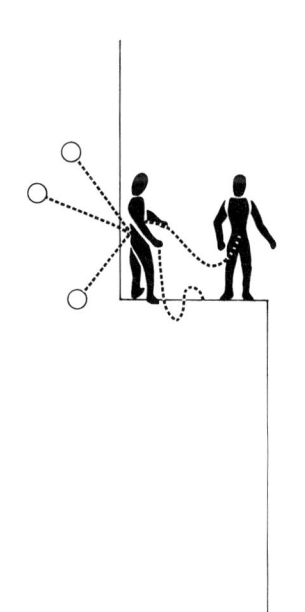

Fig 89

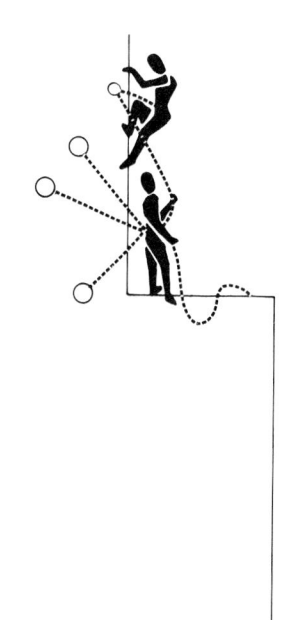

Fig 90

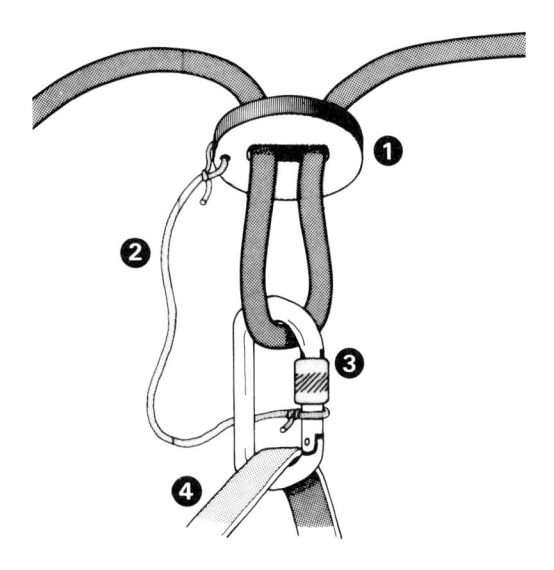

Fig 91 Belay brake for single rope (brakes with twin slots are required for double ropes). (1) Belay brake; (2) linking cord; (3) locking karabiner; (4) harness anchor/belaying loop.

Techniques

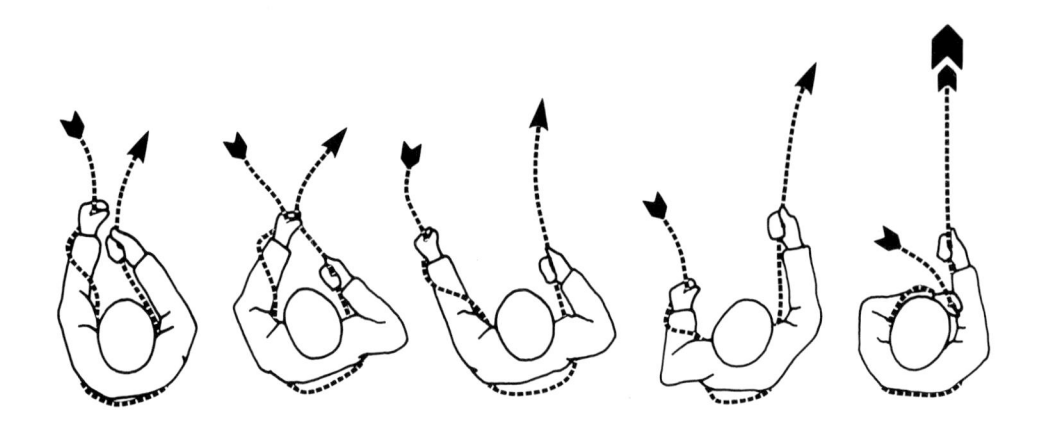

Fig 92 Waist belay. In this sequence, from left to right, the rope is being payed out to the leader (in the direction of the arrow). Drawing in rope is similar. Note that the rope is twisted only around the wrist nearest the dead or slack rope. Practise until rope can be payed out and drawn in without uncurling either hand from the rope. Note how the arm is drawn across the chest if a fall occurs (far right). The force of holding a fall will tend to rotate the body; it is important that belay anchors are arranged to resist this effect.

The golden rule when belaying is that you must not let go of the rope. Too elementary to mention? Not at all! A careless and unimaginative belayer effectively lets go of the rope every few seconds when paying out or taking in. Regardless of method used, neither hand should uncurl from the rope – at most the grip will relax slightly while the hands are repositioned.

When belaying you may or may not be forewarned of a fall. However, thanks to energy absorbing ropes, the jolt – when it comes – is rarely as severe as you might expect. (The opposite is true of a falling second, when under certain circumstances the jolt may exceed that experienced when holding a leader fall.) Provided you have arranged the stance correctly, and at some time have practised holding a simulated fall – be it that of a concrete block on a practice rig or your partner running down a grass slope – then you *will* hold that fall.

Rope Technique

PROTECTION PRINCIPLES *(Figs 94 to 97)*

The leader places protection primarily to limit the distance of a fall. It is human nature that a leader will climb close to his or her technical limit – in other words risk taking a fall – only when reliable and frequent protection is available to provide insurance in case strength or skill fails. Sometimes the leader will place protection primarily to safeguard the second. This is particularly true during traverse

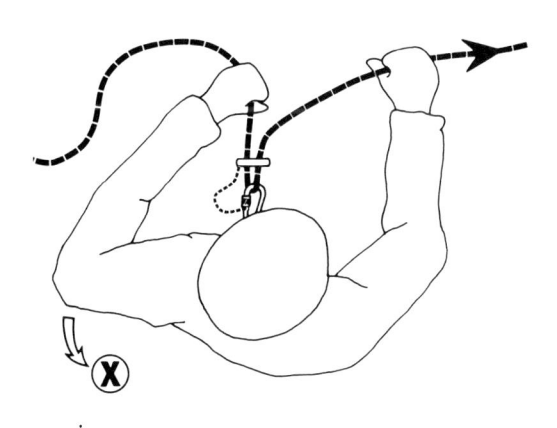

Fig 93 Belaying with a belay brake. Rope is payed out to leader (arrowed) without either hand uncurling from the rope. If a fall occurs, the braking action is initiated by drawing back the braking arm (the left in this example). Note that an obstacle at X, for example a rock bulge, would hinder this braking action; it is essential to arrange the stance so that the braking arm is not obstucted in any way. Belaying using the Italian friction hitch is similar, except that braking is initiated simply by tightening the grip in the braking hand.

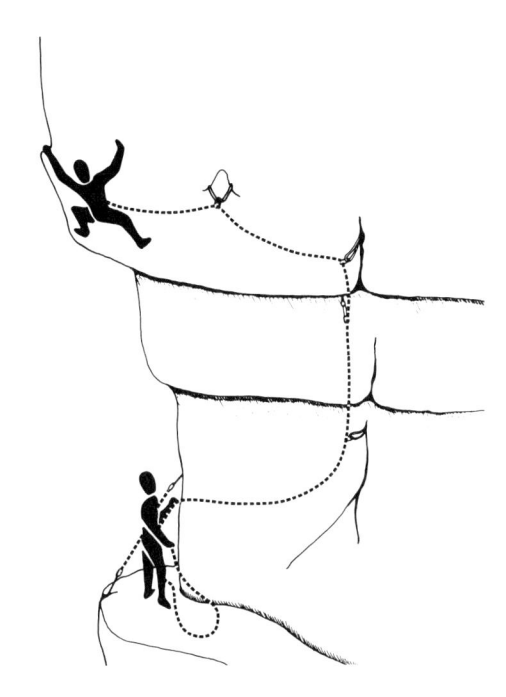

Fig 94 Leader placing runners mainly for personal safety. Note the second's 'upward pull' belay anchor aligned to resist the fall force, which will be directed from the first runner not from directly above.

Techniques

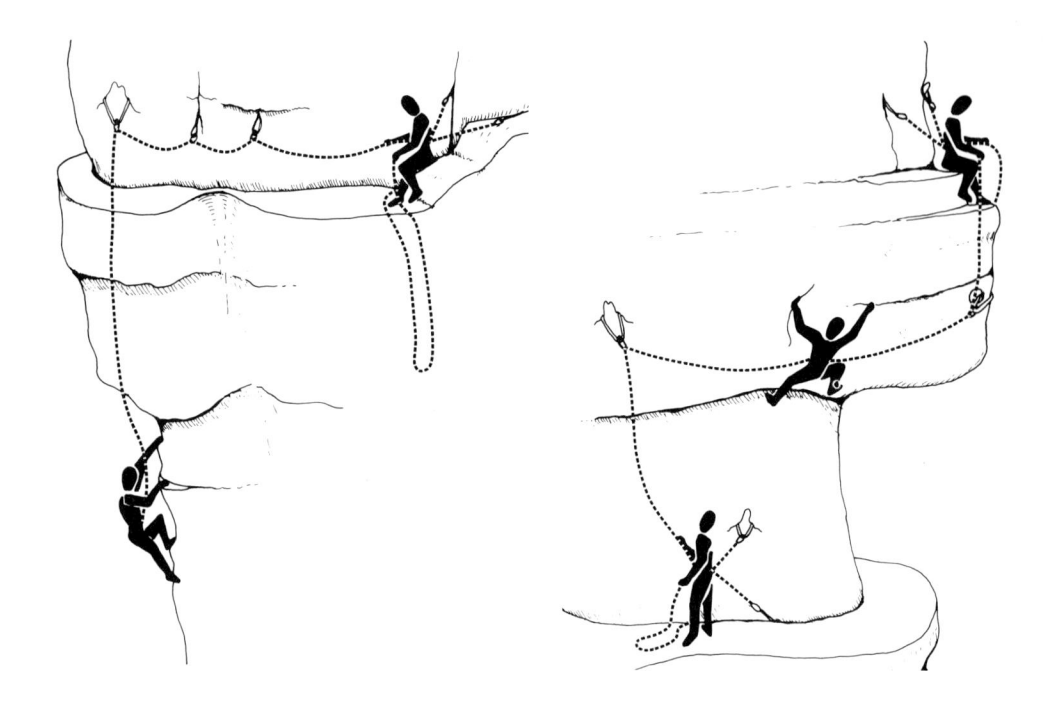

Fig 95 Runners placed mainly to protect the second. Note that the sling runner has re-routed the rope so that it pulls from directly above while the second climbs the difficult section. The runner placed on the left side of the gap in the ledge protects the leader during the awkward step across; that placed on its right protects the second when making the same move. Note the leader's sitting position to improve stability.

Fig 96 Protecting a 'middle-man'. The third climber belays the trailing rope so that the middle climber is protected during the traverse.

pitches, where the second is equally at risk from pendulum falls.

It would be a mistake to equate directly the potential seriousness of a fall with its length. Certainly the longer falls are more frightening (and more likely to culminate in collisions with ledges) but many prove less traumatic, medically and mechanically, than shorter falls sustained when no runners have been placed. For this reason theorists talk in terms of *fall factors* when describing fall severity. The factor, a number between 0 and 2, is arrived at by dividing the length of the fall by the length of rope available to absorb it (usually the distance between climber and belayer). For example, a leader who climbs above the belay ledge without placing runners and then falls off will experience a fall of factor 2 – the theoretical maximum in severity. The jolt suffered by leader and second (and their belay system) will be considerable. Conversely, the leader who slips from a

Rope Technique

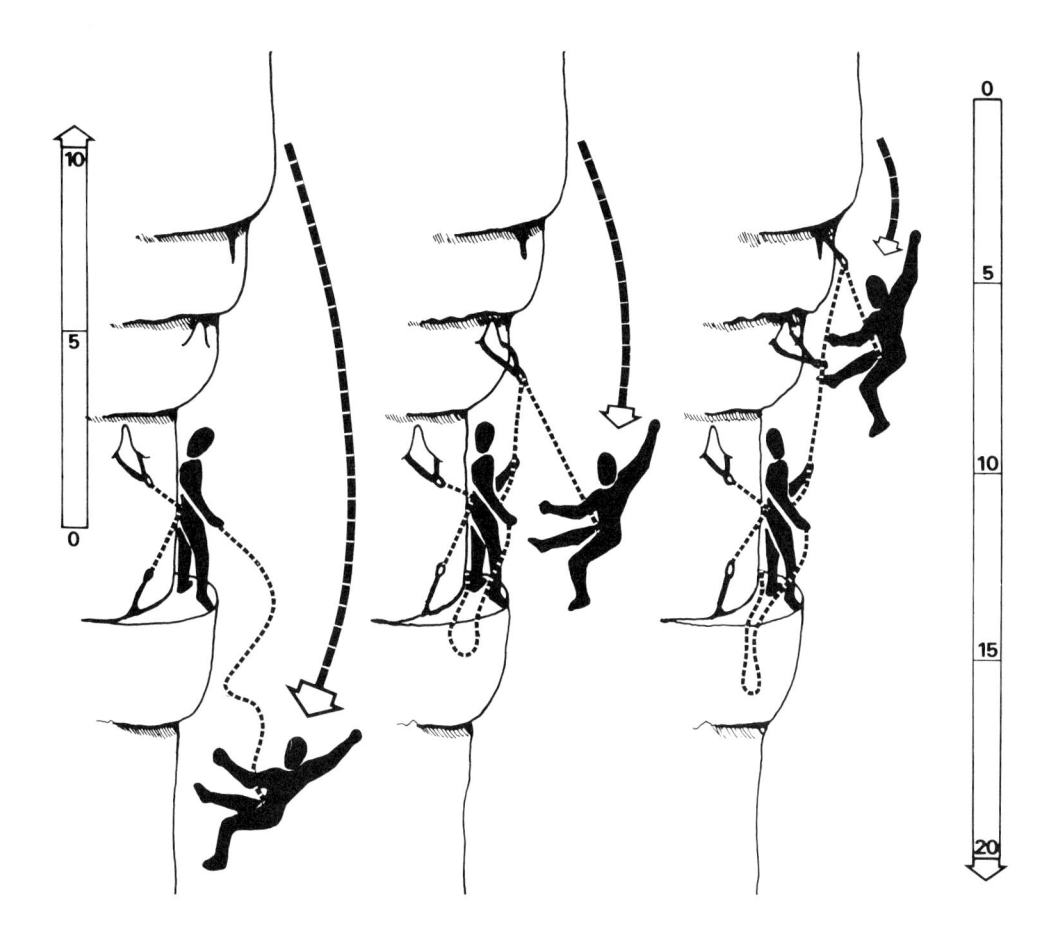

Fig 97 The fall factor increases in severity from 0 to 2. It is calculated by dividing the length of fall by the length of rope available to absorb its energy. Left: the leader has placed no protection and suffers a fall of factor 20 ÷ 10 = 2 (the maximum in severity). Centre: the sling runner placed soon after leaving the stance not only reduces the length of fall but eases the fall severity to factor 1. Right: the additional runner reduces fall severity to 0.5.

few feet above a runner when nearing the end of a pitch will experience a comparatively minor fall. The flight distance may be the same, but the severity – the fall factor – could be a tenth or less. The most important lesson fall factors teach us is the advantage of placing a runner as soon as possible after leaving the belay ledge.

Placing runners interrupts the smooth flow of movement over delicate slabs and squanders stamina on steep cracks. It is often much better to place good runners

Techniques

before reaching the difficult section so that on arrival you are able to focus your attention on solving the sequence of moves instead of fretting about lack of protection.

Alternative Rope Methods
(Figs 98 to 100)

Opportunities for protecting intricate climbs, reducing rope drag and safeguarding the second are very much greater when double ropes are used. *Figs 98 & 99* show some possibilities. Note,

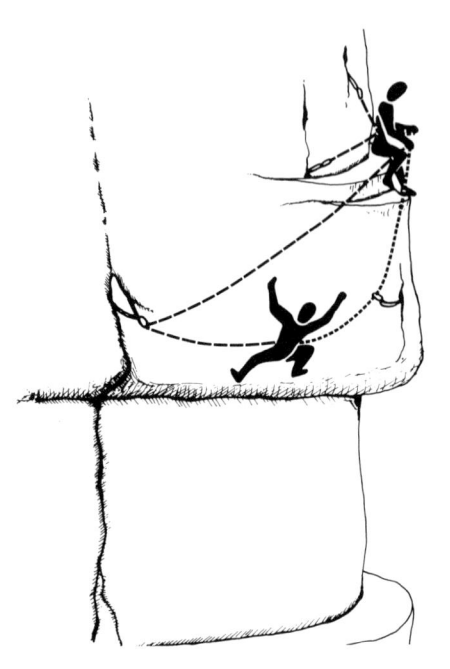

Fig 99   Double ropes can also improve protection of the second. In this case the second has left one rope clipped to a runner before the traverse to prevent a pendulum fall; the leader pays out this rope while drawing in the other. Hopefully this runner can be flicked off after the pitch has been completed.

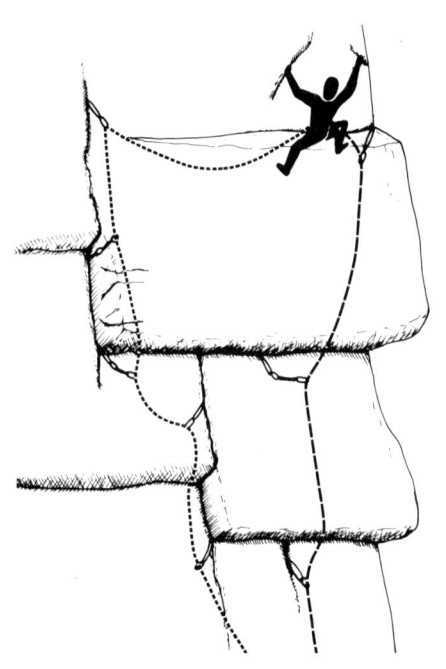

Fig 98   Double rope method. If a single rope had been used the rope drag would have proved intolerable. Note, however, that for much of the time the leader has been effectively climbing on a single thin (9mm) rope.

however, that the two ropes may become separated to such a degree that a leader fall would be held on just one of them. This is tantamount to climbing on a single 9mm rope, which is not recommended. Nevertheless, this need not present a serious problem provided runners are placed at frequent intervals (implying low fall factors).

On long but technically undemanding climbs another alternative is to treat the

Rope Technique

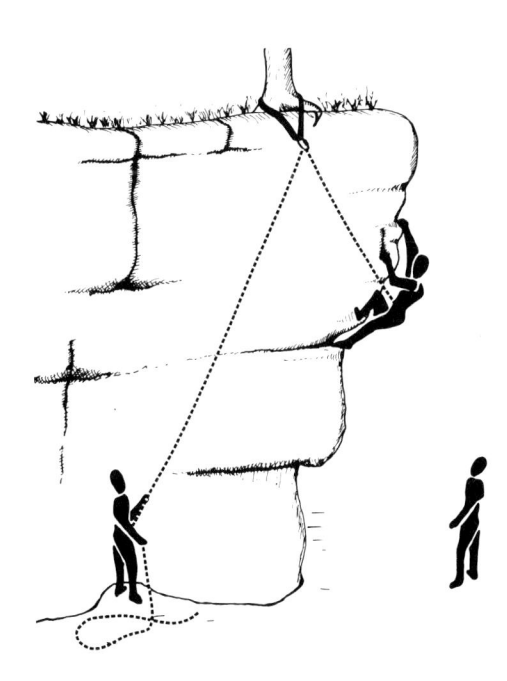

Fig 100 Top roping. An alternative to belaying from above is to clip the rope through totally reliable anchors and then belay the rope from below.

two ropes as one by clipping both into every runner, ideally in separate karabiners. This method has the speed and simplicity of single rope without sacrificing the full abseil capability and back-up security of double rope.

Rope technique in descent is essentially the reverse of that used for ascent. In this case, however, it is usual for the least able climber to descend first, placing runners for the protection of the second. Clearly this role demands some competence in route finding, placing protection and establishing a belay without supervision.

Top roping may usefully be applied on short climbs when leading is impractical (perhaps because of inexperience among the party, excessive technical difficulty, or unreliable rock). Instead of leading the climb, the belayer gains the top by other means – usually by walking around the side. After fixing belay anchors, the rope end is thrown down for others in the party to tie on and ascend in turn. Alternatively, the belayer may clip the rope into the anchors and then descend (by abseil or other means) to belay the rope from the ground. This has the advantage that the belayer can observe the attempt more closely, perhaps offering advice and encouragement.

Protection Methods

Runners which have failed – be they slings or nuts – have usually done so because the tensioning rope had flicked them out before the full force was brought to bear. The surest way to safeguard against this is to extend each of the runners at risk with an extra tape sling and karabiner. The more you can do to make the rope run in gradual curves, the better. Apart from 'protecting the protection' this also helps to reduce strength-sapping rope drag. Occasionally you will want to place a runner solely for that purpose, perhaps re-routing the rope away from a crack or overhang.

Resist the temptation to save karabiners by threading tape directly through wire runners. Wire cuts tape like a knife. Note that the plastic sleeves fitted to some wired nuts do little to alleviate the problem. Nut slings may also be used as extenders provided the second karabiner is clipped into a loop drawn from the head of the nut as shown *Fig 101*.

You might occasionally see linked

Techniques

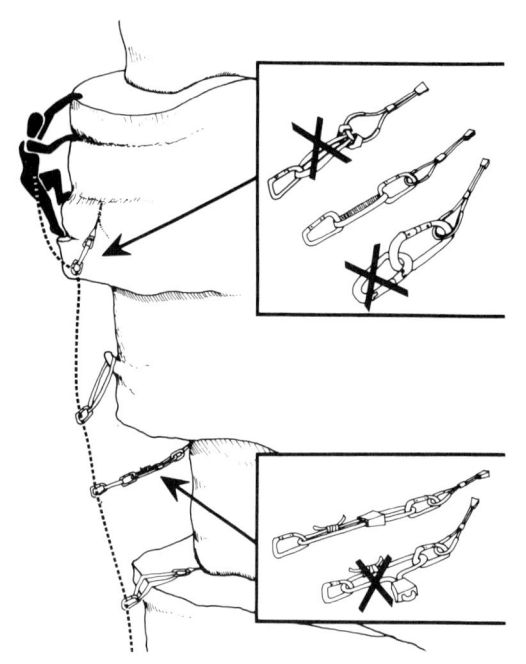

Fig 101 These runners have been extended to ease rope drag and to reduce the likelihood of them being flicked out when tensioned by the normal pull of the rope or by a fall. Note the correct methods of extending wired nuts and of improvising an extender from a nut sling.

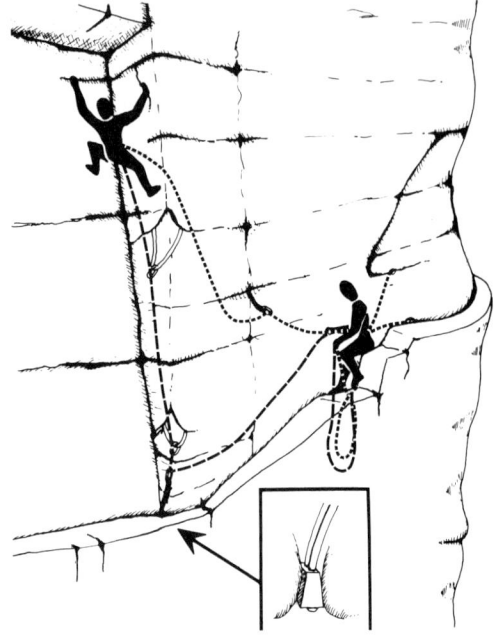

Fig 102 Protecting the protection. During a fall the runner placed at the bottom of the crack (inset) would withstand an upward pull, preventing the sling runners above from flicking off as the rope tensions.

karabiners used to extend micro-wires, but this too is unsatisfactory. The karabiners may twist against each other, perhaps allowing a gate to open and the rope to jump out. A karabiner gate may also open when pulled against a crack or protruding knob of rock. If the force of a fall applies when the gate is open in this way the karabiner could fail. Guard against this by rotating the karabiner until the gate lies outermost.

A karabiner is also severely weakened when loaded across its width (the 'minor axis'). This is most likely to occur when it has been subjected to a three-way loading, such as when the main rope is clipped directly into the karabiner which joins the two loops of a threaded tape sling. The solution to this particular problem is to lengthen the sling so that both tape loops settle at one end of the karabiner.

A persistent and cunning leader will find ways to protect even the most notoriously underprotected pitch, if necessary by calling on a fund of exotic techniques

Rope Technique

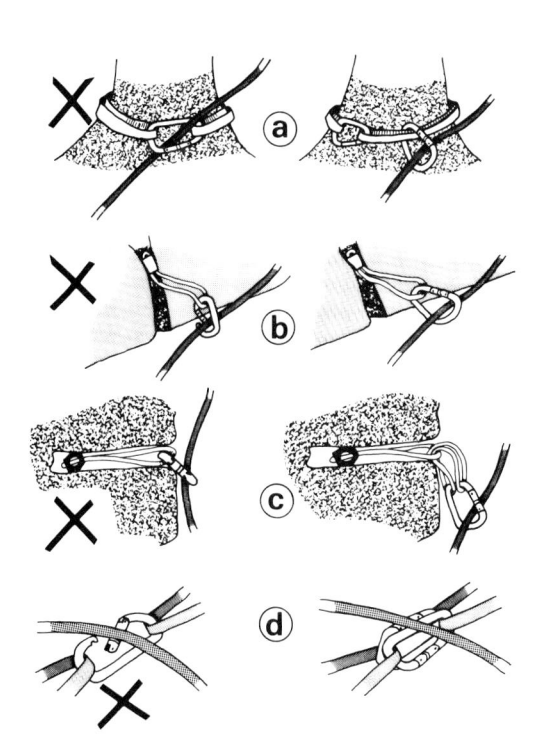

Fig 103 Positioning of karabiners.
(a) Avoid three-way loadings which stress the gate. (b) Turn karabiners so the gate will not open against the rock.
(c) Extend runners so the karabiner back bar is not stressed over an edge. (d) In the absence of locking karabiners, improvise using two ordinary karabiners with gates aligned in opposite directions.

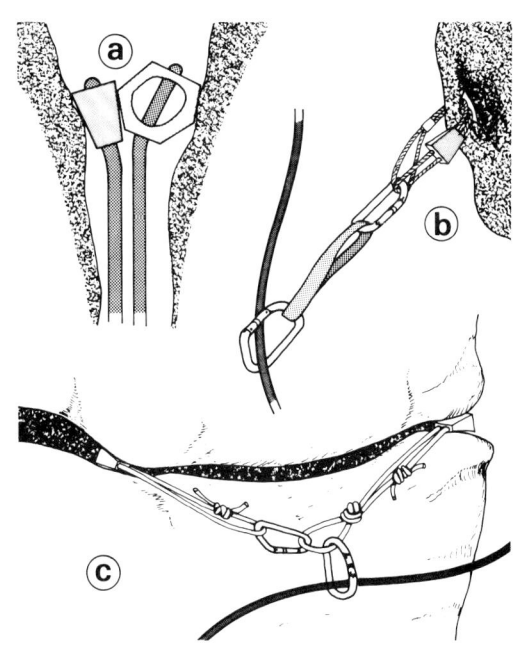

Fig 104 Advanced runner techniqes. (a) Stacked wedge and hexentric – tug hard (on one sling only) to secure. (b) Wired nut used to thread a narrow hole. Note that the karabiner clips into a loop of wire drawn from the head of the nut. (c) Nuts in opposition. The overhand knot tied in the right hand sling obtains correct tension between the two nuts. Clip opposed nuts so that if one nut fails, the rope remains captive in the other which may hold.

developed over a period of years. These might include stacked hexentrics, wire threads and opposed nuts. *Fig 104* illustrates a few of the more useful among them.

11 Emergency Rope Techniques

It is in the nature of rock climbing that emergencies will arise from time to time, no matter how careful or experienced you are. Every emergency is unique, so it is far better to grasp underlying principles than memorise a few set procedures.

ABSEILING

The technique of abseiling – sliding down fixed ropes – demands concentration and a thorough approach. There are no grey areas of forgiveness. The list of climbers killed while abseiling (it includes several famous names) makes depressing reading. Abseiling is not a game.

Applications

Abseiling, common in Alpine regions, is rarely used in Britain as a means of normal descent. However, the technique is frequently used when approaching the start of sea cliff climbs. In this case, use a spare rope if you can and leave it fixed in place – you can retrieve it after finishing the climb. In the meantime it will provide a means of escape if your route proves too difficult!

There are other occasions when you might want to abseil the full height of a cliff: when *cleaning* a potential new route (*see* Chapter 12); when researching an attempt on an established but exceptionally difficult route for which prior inspection is considered advisable; or in order to retrieve runners from a pitch on which you failed and had to be lowered off.

Circumstances sometimes dictate that the abseil rope be retrieved from below. A typical example would be an abseil from a pinnacle, or from a quarry climb which finished below a band of unstable rock. Some routes – usually *girdle traverses* – incorporate an abseil in order to bypass a difficult section. In each of these situations you may find abseil anchors (usually pitons) already fixed. That is not to say they will be reliable. Make a fresh judgement and add your own anchor if doubts remain. Remember that prolonged exposure to sunlight severely weakens tape and cord, as does the heat generated during rope retrieval. For these reasons it is essential to fit your own abseil sling on every occasion.

The foregoing are planned abseils. The need to make emergency abseils arises when climbs are abandoned because of failure, falls or bad weather. Your choice of abseil anchor will then be limited by what is immediately available and by the fact that the anchors you place will be abandoned – not that this is a time to be miserly about leaving gear behind.

Methods *(Figs 105 to 108)*

Rope friction regulates the rate of descent. Depending on the method used,

Emergency Rope Techniques

this will be generated by clothing, a friction hitch, or by the metal of a mechanical device. A certain amount of friction also develops in the controlling hand; hence the risk of sustaining rope burns unless gloves are worn.

The classic abseil, by far the most insecure and painful method, has inflicted itself on generations of mountaineers. It is none the less worth practising because it requires no special equipment other than the rope itself. *Fig 105* shows how to arrange the rope around the body – not recommended when wearing T-shirt and shorts! Take care not to lean *too* far back during the abseil, otherwise the rope under the thigh will migrate towards the knee.

A refinement of the classic abseil bypasses thigh friction (and some discomfort) using a sit sling improvised from a long tape (2.4m) and locking karabiner *(Fig 105)*. A proper sit harness takes much of the pain and uncertainty out of abseiling. Refer to the manufacturer's instructions for details of how to secure the belt and where to attach the friction device.

Purpose-made abseil devices offer the best control during the descent. These *descenders* can take a variety of forms, the most popular being the figure-of-eight design. The degree of friction obtained (and therefore the braking force) depends on rope diameter and on whether or not the rope is used single or double. When abseiling on a single 9mm rope, for instance, you will need to create additional friction by passing the slack rope around the shoulder as in a classic abseil.

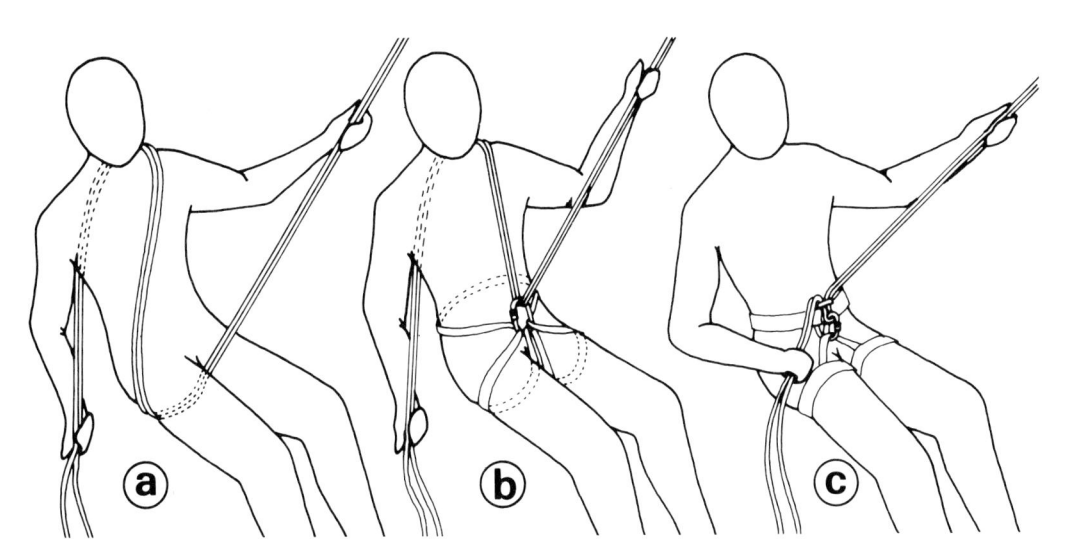

Fig 105 Abseil methods. (a) Classic. (b) Classic with improvised sit sling. (c) Sit-harness with descending device, shown here using a belay brake, but the rope arrangement and hand positions are similar when using a figure-of-eight descender or Italian friction hitch.

Techniques

Fig 106

Fig 107

Fig 106   Figure-of-eight descender.

Fig 107   Italian friction hitch with HMS locking karabiner.

Fig 108   Belay brake with locking karabiner.

Fig 108

Emergency Rope Techniques

Although mechanical devices are inherently safer than traditional methods of abseiling, take great care not to let clothing or hair be drawn into the device. The disadvantage of the descender is that it is an extra item of equipment to buy and carry.

The Italian friction hitch makes an excellent alternative to the descender and costs nothing. Arrange the ropes through the locking karabiner (ideally of the HMS type) in the same way as for belaying and control the descent as you would when using a descender.

Belay brakes are frequently used for abseiling despite a jerky descent and risk of overheating (a karabiner back bar inserted between brake and locking karabiner will act as a spacer and help smooth the descent). Other improvised abseil devices (linked karabiners, brake bars, etc.) are more complicated and less foolproof than either Italian friction hitch or belay brake and may now be regarded as obsolete.

Abseil Anchors *(Fig 109)*

Abseil ropes placed directly around a block or spike rarely retrieve satisfactorily. Instead, fit a sling over the anchor point and thread the abseil rope directly through this (there is no need to sacrifice a karabiner). If necessary, extend the sling to clear obstructions and give trouble-free retrieval.

Place abseil anchors as you would belay anchors, paying equal attention to the quality of placements. Remember that the anchors will only be as good as their ability to withstand a force coming from the direction indicated by the lie of the ropes. In this respect it is particularly

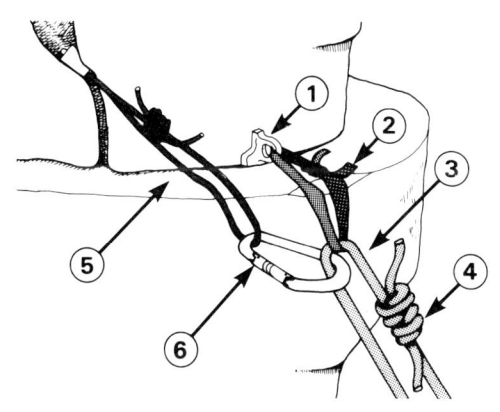

Fig 109 *Abseil anchor precautions. (1) Insert piton for maximum mechanical advantage (no possibility of swivelling out). (2) Place abseil anchor sling over rounded edge; if necessary use peg hammer to knock off sharp edges. (3) Make abseil anchor sling of sufficient length to clear obstructions. (4) Join double ropes using double fisherman's knot. (5) Insure the main anchor with a back-up anchor, usually removed by last person prior to descent. (6) Clip the back-up anchor into the abseil ropes so that it does not share the load, but if both anchors are to be abandoned fix the slings so that the load is shared equally between them.*

important to use a spike set high above the ledge to eliminate the possibility of the abseil anchor sling lifting off.

A safety rope protects practice abseils. Arrange this precisely as you would a top rope and simply pay out rope instead of taking in. As a precaution use a separate set of belay anchors from those used to

Techniques

anchor the abseil rope.

In a genuine abseil situation you may not have sufficient rope or time to arrange a safety rope. An alternative is to fix one or more back-up anchors. The last person to abseil will remove these prior to descent, secure in the knowledge that the main anchor has proved itself reliable. For a true test, carefully adjust the length of back-up anchors so they do not quite support any of the load but would do so without being jolted if the main anchor failed.

The Descent

As a precaution, secure yourself to the anchors while preparing the abseil. Now draw the rope through the abseil anchor sling until the mid-point is reached (but join double ropes with a double fisherman's knot after threading the sling). When using double ropes make a mental note of which rope to pull down during retrieval otherwise the knot will foul the sling.

Tie rope ends together using a bulky knot before feeding them down the crag. If all else fails this knot will stop you from sliding off the end. Avoid tangles by throwing over just a few coils of rope and then feeding out the rest hand over hand. Consider weighting the ends if a strong wind is blowing, otherwise they may whip across the cliff and snag somewhere out of reach.

After fitting the abseil device, but before launching over the edge, check once more that harness buckles and locking karabiners are fastened correctly. There's no coming back! Abseil anchors placed low or towards the rear of the ledge are most likely to fail during the first stage of the descent; if necessary creep over the edge so the rope will not pull at the anchors from a high angle.

The worst moment in abseiling is stepping over the edge. Once established on steep rock and committed to the descent you will feel less apprehensive. Before resuming the descent, check that the ropes do not lie over a sharp edge or in a crack where they may jam during retrieval. When ready, release a little rope through the controlling hand until you are leaning backwards with feet flat against the rock. Avoid the spectacular leaping descent favoured in public demonstrations (which impresses onlookers but places additional strain on the anchors) and simply walk backwards down the rock, feet apart, while regulating the rate of descent by adjusting the position and grip of the control hand. Note that the upper hand merely aids balance and does not grip the rope.

If you need to pause for more than a few seconds it is useful to know how to lock off a descender (or Italian friction hitch) temporarily. The simplest method is to gather up a loop of slack rope and form it into a simple hitch around the taut rope above the descender. A belay brake is more difficult to lock off because you lose friction while raising the loop of slack rope. Instead, try twisting the slack rope around your leg.

A prusik loop fixed around both abseil ropes and attached to your harness will act as a 'dead man's handle' and arrest your fall if for some reason – such as being struck by a falling stone – you let go of the rope. In these circumstances the klemheist knot is more likely to lock quickly than the standard prusik knot. The upper hand grips the knot during

Emergency Rope Techniques

Fig 110 Abseil practice using a safety rope. The belayer pays out rope in the normal way; use separate anchors for belayer and abseil rope. Note the body position of the abseiler: leaning back, with feet apart.

Techniques

descent, sliding it down to prevent locking. Make sure the loop is not so long that when locked the knot rises beyond reach.

Rope Retrieval

As first climber to descend during a multiple abseil retreat, you will fix the next abseil anchor and secure yourself to it *before* releasing the abseil ropes. Before the last person descends a trial retrieval of a half-metre or so will indicate whether or not the ropes will pull down freely. If not, ask for the anchor sling to be rearranged and try again. The last person down will take care not to relinquish the rope ends if there is a chance that they may swing out of reach. After untying the bulky knot, the ropes are recovered by pulling down on the appropriate rope end. Watch out for falling stones when the rope finally pulls free.

Twisting is the most likely cause of jammed ropes during retrieval. Confirm this by holding the ropes apart and flicking them away from the rock. If after this the rope still refuses to move, the knot may have jammed in a crack. On a one-shot abseil you now have the option of abandoning the rope and returning to free it later. On a long descent, however, you may have no choice but to reascend the ropes on prusik loops and rearrange the abseil. Note that each of these prusik knots must be tied around *both* ropes. It is dangerous to tie off one rope and prusik up the other; under load the slight sawing action of the rope could melt the anchor sling. No easy solution exists to the nightmare problem of a rope which jams part-way through retrieval when one end has passed from reach.

PRUSIKING

The term prusiking applies to any one of several methods of ascending fixed rope. The principle common to all is a one-way knot or device which can slide up the rope but locks when loaded.

Applications

A rare but important application of prusiking is in regaining the route after a fall which leaves you hanging in space or among unclimbable rock. It may be possible to improvise loops from gear you happen to have with you, but it would be better to carry prusik loops already made up into suitable lengths. The second may also resort to prusiking if called upon to complete a difficult pitch in darkness or bad weather. As already indicated, you may be forced to prusik back up an abseil rope if all other attempts to free it have failed.

Methods *(Figs 111 and 112)*

The standard prusik knot (*see* Chapter 7) is versatile and, with practice, is easy to tie one-handed. However, it may fail to work properly in some circumstances – abseil protection, improvised prusiking on tape slings, etc. The klemheist knot is a useful alternative in these situations, particularly since friction can be increased simply by adding extra turns in the knot. There are several other variants, each with special advantages, but these two knots will meet most needs. Except in special circumstances, such as big wall climbing, the superior efficiency of mechanical prusik devices fails to justify the extra weight and expense.

Emergency Rope Techniques

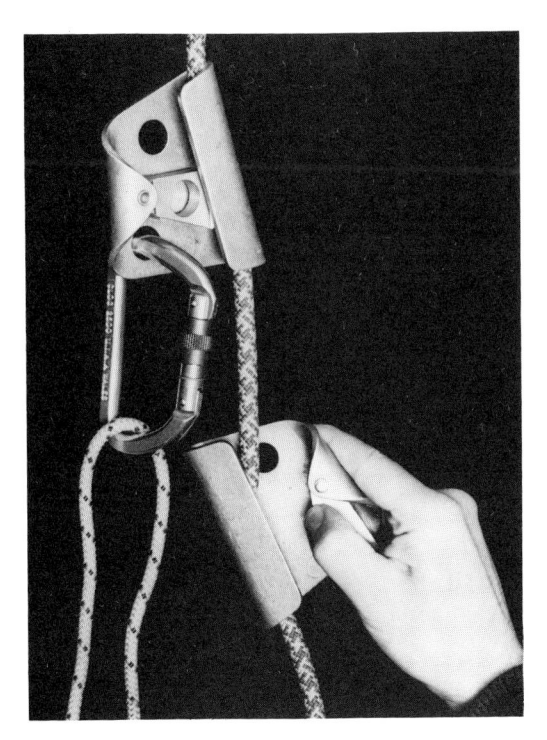

Fig 111 Clog ascenders (mechanical prusik devices).

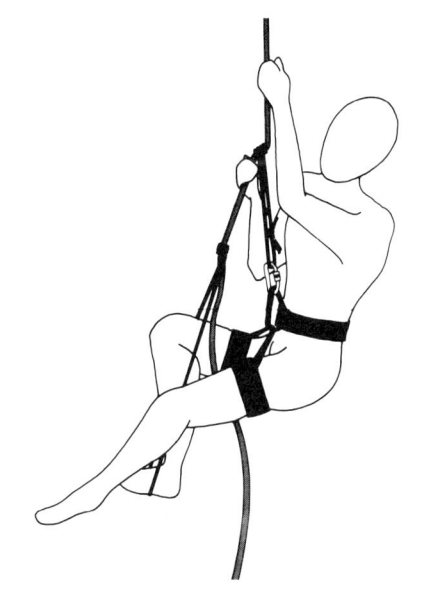

Fig 112 Ascending a rope using prusik loops. Note that the loop attached to the harness is uppermost.

To ascend a fixed rope, first knot both prusik loops to the rope. Attach the short loop to the harness by a locking karabiner, but leave the longer one free as a foot loop. Note that the short loop is fixed uppermost; this ensures that the rope is in tension (from the foot loop) while raising the knot. The other foot assists the ascent by fending off the rock while you progress slowly upwards.

Sometimes a prusik knot will slip under load, perhaps because of mud on the rope or because the cord diameter is too large. Unless the slide is stopped the loop will melt through – with catastrophic results. Guard against this by tying overhand knots in the slack rope beneath you after every few metres of ascent. The same precaution safeguards against slipping cams on mechanical devices.

A prusik loop must never be subjected to a shock load. A fall of less than one metre may be sufficient to cause failure. For this reason it is futile to protect a solo ascent by sliding a prusik loop up a fixed rope as you climb. Chapter 12 suggests a more reliable method using a mechanical prusik device.

The best place to practise prusiking and discover its limitations is on a fixed rope hung from a tree branch. Only by experimenting with various methods in this safe situation will you resolve the problems that will arise in a real emergency.

Techniques

FAILURES AND FALLS

A complex retreat after a failure or fall will involve lowers and abseils, demanding ingenuity and a good grasp of the principles of rope security. Some typical situations are described below. A further haunting possibility is the fall which results in serious injury, requiring medical attention and evacuation by a mountain rescue team.

Lowering

Lowering a fallen or failed second down to a resting ledge will cause few problems provided your stance is braced and you are using a belay brake or Italian friction hitch. Lowering a leader involves even less effort because of additional friction developed at the runner karabiner. However, lowering someone from a waist belay can be quite painful when wearing light clothing.

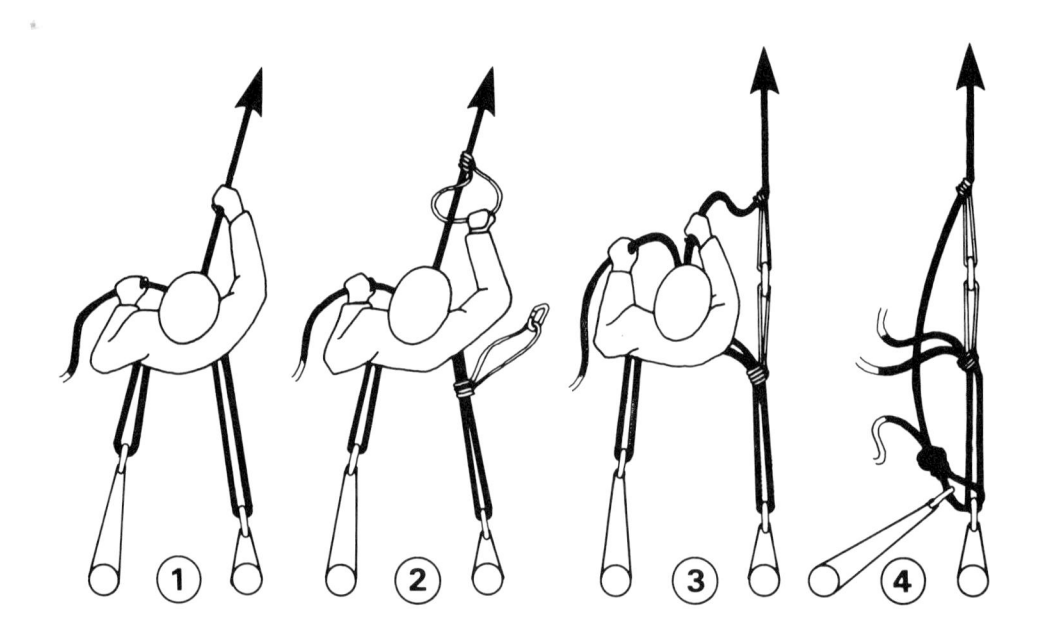

Fig 113   Escaping the belay system. (1) Hold the fall. (2) Attach prusik loops to the live rope and, if necessary, to the anchor ropes. (3) Secure the prusik loop to the anchor and pay out rope until the load transfers to the anchor. (4) Untie from the rope and back up the prusik loop with the main rope and subsidiary anchors.

Emergency Rope Techniques

When lowering (or reversing) after a failed lead you may want to retrieve protection as you go, thereby abandoning only the top runner and karabiner. When using a single rope this leaves you without back-up if the top runner fails. It may be wiser simply to lower off and retrieve the runners later from an abseil. On no account try to save a karabiner by lowering on a rope threaded directly through the runner. The sling will melt and break.

When using double ropes you can take advantage of the system by lowering on one rope while being belayed on the other as you remove protection.

If failure occurs high on a pitch (i.e. with insufficient rope available for the lower) the leader may be forced to abseil from the top runner. If the top runner is not totally reliable then a partial lower could be made to reach a better abseil anchor further down.

Escaping the System *(Fig 113)*

In the event of serious injury after a fall the belayer may need to secure the rope directly to the anchors and escape the system – either to descend to give assistance and first aid or to go for help.

The first priority is to transfer the load from your belay device to the anchors. First fix a prusik loop around the live rope, then clip this, extended if necessary, into a nearby anchor karabiner. If none are within reach, fix a second prusik loop around the anchor ropes and link the two loops with a karabiner. That done, gently lower the fallen climber until the load transfers through the prusik loop to the anchors. Before releasing the belay, reinforce the prusik loop by tying a knot in the slack rope and clipping it directly into the anchors. Now you are free to untie from the rope.

Your next action depends on the nature of the emergency and the amount of spare rope available. If using double ropes, or if the fallen climber hangs less than half a rope length below, you will have sufficient rope to be able to abseil down and give assistance. If not, you may be forced to reverse prusik, probably using the klemheist knot with additional turns to improve grip on the taut rope.

First-aid Checklist

Check Breathing
If necessary clear airway using a hooked finger to remove obstructions – vomit, blood, teeth etc. Turn casualty to lie in the recovery position (unless you suspect spinal injury). This helps to maintain a clear airway.

Check for Severe Bleeding
Apply direct pressure from a pad to stop bleeding. Elevate the limb.

Check for Broken Bones
Do not move the casualty if a spinal injury is suspected. Immobilise other fractures using improvised splints and slings.

Monitor Condition
Keep casualty warm and comfortable while awaiting rescue (protect from wind and insulate from ground). Reassure casualty and monitor condition regularly.

Techniques

First Aid and Rescue

There is little point in learning elaborate rescue techniques unless you aim to join a local team, but you will learn a great deal that is useful by enrolling on a first-aid course. Here you will learn how to examine for fractures and dislocations, to recognise the symptoms of internal injury, and to apply basic treatment. Each year a special course is held on first aid for climbers; the British Mountaineering Council will have details. Meanwhile the checklist given on page 103 will serve as a reminder.

The International Distress Signal indicates your need of help: *six successive whistle blasts or torch flashes repeated after a one-minute pause.* The acknowledging response from approaching rescuers will be three blasts or flashes repeated after a one-minute pause. However, if someone can be spared from attending to the casualty time will be saved by sending them down to the valley to seek help directly – either from a rescue post (locations marked on some maps) or by dialling 999 and asking for mountain rescue. It is very important that details of the casualty's injuries and precise location on the crag can be supplied at this stage. The requirements are summarised in the checklist.

Rescue teams comprise local volunteers trained in first aid and evacuation techniques. When there is need for urgent medical attention the team may be assisted by an RAF rescue helicopter. In this case someone from the rescue team

To Alert Mountain Rescue

Dial 999, ask for police/mountain rescue, and have the following written details ready:

- **Name and description of injured person.**
- **Precise position of the injured person on the crag.**
- **Location of the crag, including grid reference and map sheet number.**
- **Time and nature of accident.**
- **Extent of injuries.**
- **Indication of prevailing weather at the scene (cloud base, wind strength, visibility, and so on).**

Remain by the phone until met by a police officer or member of the rescue team.

Rescue Helicopters

- **Secure all loose equipment before arrival of the helicopter (weight rucksacks, jackets etc. with stones).**
- **Identify yourself by raising your arms in a V as the helicopter approaches. Do *not* wave.**
- **Protect the injured person from the rotor downdraught (which is intense).**
- **Allow the winchman to land of his own accord.**
- **Do not approach the helicopter unless directed to do so by one of the crew, as there is danger from rotors, exhaust, etc.**

will advise bystanders of correct procedure as the helicopter approaches. If the helicopter arrives first, follow the standard precautions given in the checklist.

When climbing as a party of two on a remote cliff you may be forced into the unenviable position of having to make a choice between staying with your companion and hoping your signals are answered, attempting an improvised rescue, or of leaving to seek help directly. Improvised rescue of a seriously injured climber may do more harm than good. In most cases it would be better to secure your companion from further falls, administer first aid, protect from wind and cold, and then seek expert assistance. Naturally an exception may have to be made if an accident occurred in a very remote area. If planning such a trip you should practise improvised techniques, for example hoists and tragsitz lowers. Refer to the bibliography for further reading.

12 Some Special Topics

This chapter introduces some fascinating aspects of the sport which lie outside the mainstream interest. It can do so only in the broadest terms, dipping occasionally into the underlying philosophy or highlighting some special technique. A full treatment would demand a book in itself.

FIRST ASCENTS

Historians describe rock climbing in terms of pivotal discovery – new routes, new crags, new techniques. Ordinary climbers, quite rightly, are not so much preoccupied with the antics of the 'rock stars' as their own fulfilment in the sport. Nevertheless, most of us will produce a new climb or variant at some time – perhaps on impulse, possibly even by accident. Few major first ascents, however, are made without considerable research and preparatory effort. This is half the fun: even the grottiest little route achieves stature in day-dreams.

The actual climb will unfold much as usual, except that the uncertainty of the outcome will add poignancy to the drama. Perhaps the most unexpected revelation is that motivation, charged beforehand by ambition and a secret yearning for fame, has switched and now responds to a physical dynamo. You want to succeed because success will make your head buzz for a couple of hours and glow for a couple of days. Who needs confirmation from a two-line entry in a magazine or guidebook?

Practical Aspects

Hundreds of low standard first ascents await those with a pioneering bent and stoical attitude towards loose rock and vegetation. Most will be unearthed from among the rambling buttresses of remote mountain crags; simply pick your line and let the adventure commence.

Opportunities for *on sight* first ascents of major unclimbed lines are rare. At these high levels of technical difficulty, crack debris and lichenous rock will defeat the purist approach. The usual remedy is to abseil down the proposed line, cleaning as you go with a wire brush and other tools of the trade. Naturally this also gives you an opportunity to log the location of crucial holds and maybe even to pull on one or two to see what they feel like. Who knows, you might also test-fit a couple of runners, perhaps leaving one in place to save precious strength on the actual attempt. All this is very industrious, but pioneering it is not. The irony is that a new route climbed by these tactics involves less uncertainty than an established route climbed by following a guidebook description.

Nevertheless, if your route proves to be a worthwhile addition to the crag people will want to know about it. Dissemination of new route information is a four-part process: *immediate* – by bragging to your mates (guaranteeing next day repeats); *quick* – via the new route log at a nearby hut, cafe, pub, or gear shop (encouraging connoisseur interest and re-

Fig 114 An aid climb on Kilnsey Crag, Yorkshire.

peat ascents by local activists); *slow* – through the pages of the monthly magazines (impressing relatives but few others); and *slow-but-sure* – through the considered prose of the guide writer.

AID CLIMBING *(Fig 114)*

Aid climbing differs fundamentally from free climbing in that it makes unnatural progress up the route. It has to be said that standing in slings and pulling up on pitons is not everyone's idea of a good time, but to be fair it will take you into spectacular situations unattainable by conventional means. Except when practised at its extreme, it is a relatively safe, if laborious, way to climb.

Climbers traditionally took up aid climbing during the winter months when the weather was too cold or wet for enjoyable free climbing. During the 1970s, however, most aid climbers defected to indoor walls or to ice climbing.

The aid climber, ponderous in chains of karabiners and pitons, suffers an uneasy existence in the vibrant company of the free climber. Ethically the two pursuits are at opposite ends of the spectrum. In practice they overlap on certain routes once aided but now 'free climbed' by an assortment of questionable techniques (derisively referred to as *frigging*).

Techniques

Aid climbers once dangled and whacked with impunity among gritstone quarries and limestone outcrops. Nowadays these crags provide high quality free climbs and consequently the opportunities for aid climbing are severely limited. All that remain are a few of the more spectacular roof climbs which so far have repulsed free attempts. Internationally the story is much the same, the more notable exceptions being the vast overhangs of the Dolomites and the blankest walls of Yosemite.

Aid Placements *(Figs 115 & 116)*

Aiding on nuts not only saves time and effort but inflicts far less damage on the rock than banging in pitons. The short, stiff loops of wired nuts ensure maximum height gain per placement – an important consideration on long routes. Placing aid differs little from placing protection, except that now you must steel yourself and trust marginal placements. This is not as alarming as it sounds because of the frequency of protection.

Pitons (also known as *pegs*) are still used for fine, flared or roof cracks where nuts will not hold. Forged from hard steel, they consist of a blade or wedge plus karabiner hole. Blade thickness varies from the wafer thin *rurps* to fist sized *bongs*. Pitons are fixed in place using a peg hammer.

Skill and ingenuity in piton placement develop with practice. The ideal placement – and the one sought when using pitons for belay anchors or protection on free climbs – will be made in a deep fault, as opposed to a cracked block or flake, in such a way that the plane of the blade is at right angles to the direction of pull.

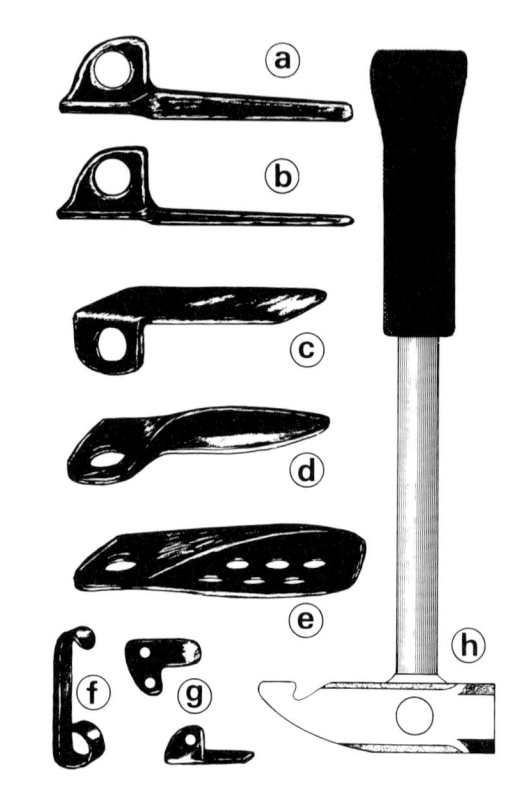

Fig 115 Pitons: (a) kingpin (thick); (b) kingpin (thin); (c) offset knifeblade; (d) angle; (e) bong; (f) skyhook; (g) rurps; (h) peg hammer.

However, when placing pitons for progress (which merely have to sustain body weight) you must be prepared to use all manner of cracks and pockets, perhaps resorting to stacked or tied off pitons if nothing else will fit.

When selecting a piton, aim to push fit the first two-thirds of its length so that only the final third needs to be hammered home. A twanging noise when hammering indicates that the crack is shallow and the piton has hit bottom. You might

Some Special Topics

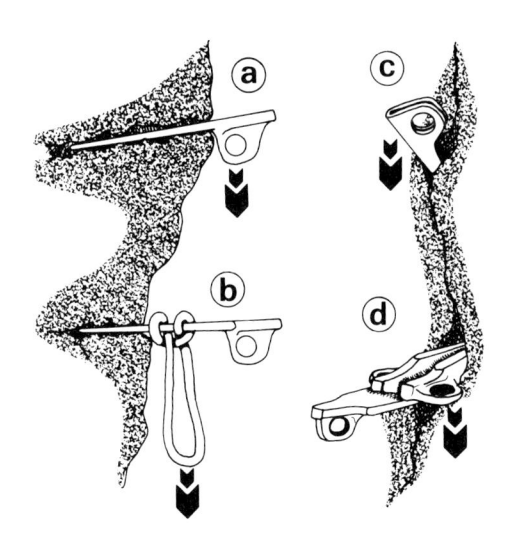

Fig 116 Piton placements: (a) Good placement: mechanically sound and fully inserted. (b) Long piton tied off with clove hitch to reduce leverage. (c) Good placement in vertical crack: constriction below piton. (d) Stacked kingpins as poor substitute for Angle piton. In this example, maintain tension in the stack by clipping only the right-hand piton.

choose another site, select a shorter piton, or tie off the existing one to reduce leverage using a clove hitch tied in a short sling.

Piton extraction is a skill in itself. First loosen the placement by hitting the piton eye from side to side (to make the blade swivel). You may now be able to lift out the piton with your fingers. If not, insert the hammer spike or extraction notch and prise out the piton as you would a nail. Problems arise if the blade has bent inside the crack, or if you are unable to hammer the eye from both directions. One solution is to clip a karabiner into the piton and pull outwards on this while carefully tapping the eye.

Popular aid climbs are frequently found *pegged up*, meaning that most if not all placements are already fixed in place. Such routes are fast to climb, provided you have the nerve to trust your weight to rotting slings and rusting metal!

Some of the more spectacular and overhanging routes are climbed almost entirely on bolts drilled into blank rock. Doubtless these outings will remain popular until such time as the bolt hangers finally disintegrate, but we can expect no more of the genre. Not only would the creation of new bolt routes entail days of effort, but it would attract a storm of protest from ethically minded climbers. Occasionally new bolts are placed from abseil for belay anchors or protection on free climbs, but the practice is generally frowned upon by those who regard bolts as a threat to the delicate balance of power which exists between belligerent climber and unyielding rock.

The Aid Climbing Sequence

When transferring to the next aid point your weight is taken in short tape ladders (*etriers*), whereas when stationary you may sit in relative comfort supported by the harness which in turn is clipped to the aid point by a short length of cord (*cow's tail*). Often two cow's tails are used: one short, one long. On a multi-pitch route, and despite extra tangles, you might secure both etriers to your harness with safety lines. Peg hammers are *always* secured in this way – a precaution your

Techniques

vulnerable second will appreciate.

Ten seconds' delay in one stage of the transfer process amounts to more than fifteen minutes overall in a climb which involves a hundred aid points. Multiply that by the dozen or so stages involved in each cycle and it is easy to see why benightments are common. On a multi-pitch or multi-day route the second will save time by prusiking up a fixed rope (using mechanical prusik devices) to remove gear.

Only those climbers with orderly minds will excel at aid climbing. The first priority is to rack equipment so that it is accessible. A bandoleer slung across the shoulder is most convenient. For optimum speed in selection and placement, try grouping wires on a single karabiner but racking pitons individually. Avoid tangles by relegating tie-offs and extension slings to the harness gear loops.

Orderliness extends to the process of transferring from one placement to the next. This particular ten-point plan is aimed at conserving energy:

1. Stand in the highest rungs of the etriers while fixing the next placement (a short cow's tail maintains balance).
2. Clip chain of two karabiners into new placement.
3. Transfer one etrier to new placement (clip into lower karabiner of the chain).
4. Raise unsupported foot to stand in lowest rung of top etrier (weight still mainly supported by old placement).
5. Clip main rope into upper karabiner of old placement (this now becomes a runner).
6. Gradually transfer weight to top etrier.
7. Remove short cow's tail from old placement then clip long cow's tail into lower karabiner of new placement and sit back on its support.
8. Retrieve bottom etrier and transfer it to lower karabiner of new placement alongside top etrier.
9. Climb up etriers to stand in highest rungs and clip in short cow's tail to maintain balance.
10. Fix next placement.

At this stage you may not be able to visualise those movements, but it will make sense if you have tried aid climbing and struggled in vain to find a consistent transfer process. Note that the method makes optimum use of the cow's tails, minimises the fall distance if a placement fails, and cuts down on unproductive movements. For all that it is only a guideline. You might use it as a starting point from which to develop your own system. In general, try to satisfy these fundamental principles: maximum efficiency in movement, preservation of strength, minimum strain on placements.

ALPINE ROCK

Not all Alpine climbing revolves around snow peaks and glaciers. The limestone walls of the Dolomites, for instance, or the granite pillars of the Mont Blanc massif, present magnificent rock climbing challenges set amid breathtaking scenery.

Risk and Reward

Imagine, if you can, looking up a thousand-metre wall of near-vertical limestone: twenty-five pitches of climbing. Facing north, the wall weeps with snow melt from yesterday's storm. It is 7 a.m. The summit rocks glow red in the dawn light. Rocks loosed from frost descend in a screaming volley, sparking at each impact and releasing their sulphurous smell. Despite the danger, you sag from the belay anchors through lack of sleep and surfeit of cheap wine.

The climbing begins, but it brings no comfort. The rock is cold to the touch, its holds treacherously loose. Your stiff soled boots feel clumsy on the holds, while the rucksack – heavy with food and emergency equipment – tugs at your shoulders.

Fifteen pitches later, little has changed. Infrequent protection and complex route finding add to the anxiety. An hour has passed since you last saw an *in situ* piton confirming your position. On a nearby peak the clouds thicken, swirling themselves into an afternoon storm. A rumble of thunder confirms your fears. After fifteen minutes of futile struggle with poor belay anchors you call down to your second to begin climbing but not to fall off. This is nothing new; at times both of you have been climbing at once, fifty metres apart, because the leader failed to find any belay anchors worth tying to.

It is your lead again. It could be the twentieth, but you have lost count. A leaning prow soars upwards into the clouds; the thought of clinging to its crest makes you gasp, but the limestone is as solid as concrete. With sudden strength you find yourself swarming from hold to hold, the rope snaking beneath like a kite string. Neither storm nor darkness will stop you now.

Night came at the summit. That was five hours ago. Now you are spinning gently in space at the rope ends, hoping somehow to regain rock and fix an anchor for your fifth consecutive abseil. The torch beam empties itself into darkness.

By pushing and swinging you finally come to land on a foothold. The outlook is not good: it is the middle of the night; you are perched on a book-sized ledge half-way up an unknown wall in a foreign country, and your survival depends on finding an anchor from which to continue the descent. Beneath a small overlap the torch spotlights a piton choked with abseil cord, confirming that others have gone this way. The flood of relief is overwhelming. Life has never felt so good.

Equipment and Techniques
(Figs 117 & 118)

Provided no snow and ice climbing is involved, you will base your equipment for a one-day Alpine rock climb on what you might take for a long mountaineering route in Britain. Unfortunately these one-day Alpine routes have a nasty habit of dragging on into the night.

The classic dilemma is whether or not to take bivouac gear, the implication being that time lost in carrying it invites benightment. At the very least you should aim to carry a survival bag and spare pullovers (or quilted jacket) against the possibility of storm enforced delay.

A primary consideration will be choice of footwear. Friction boots are fine for short routes at low altitude, but not for long climbs which might include snowfields on the approach or descent. Mountain boots are clumsy for technical climbing, however, so a good compromise

Techniques

might be a lightweight but stiff soled *kletterschuhe*.

You can afford to relax ethics a little for the big rock routes. Pitons are used frequently for belay and abseil anchors. As a rule you would carry a selection of six or seven pitons, plus two or three in reserve for a forced retreat. Abseil anchor slings can be cut as and when required from a 5m length of 7mm cord carried specifically for the purpose. You might substitute a short-handled ice hammer for the peg hammer if snow is expected. Although clumsy to carry on rock, this will save having to carry a separate ice-axe.

Paradoxically, British climbers invite disaster in the Alps with their thorough and unhurried approach to belaying learned on little crags. Speed *is* important in the Alps. Two techniques which help maintain the momentum of the ascent are *direct belaying* and *moving together*.

Direct Belaying

In direct belaying, the Italian friction hitch is tied directly into a locking karabiner at the anchor. Meanwhile the belayer secures to a separate anchor. Although the direct belay can be used to safeguard the leader, its main application is in keeping pace with an athletic second racing up a simple pitch. It goes without saying that the anchor must be 100 per cent reliable.

Moving Together

The technique of moving together is most useful when crossing easy ground between pitches of more difficult climbing – the sort of rock you might climb solo but for the inconvenience of having to untie the ropes. Each climber takes up coils until separated by 5–10m of rope (the actual length will depend on the nature of terrain). These coils are carried over the shoulder in the normal way, except that the final turn is tied off at the harness using a figure-of-eight knot (to prevent the rest of the coils becoming a noose). After taking up a couple of short

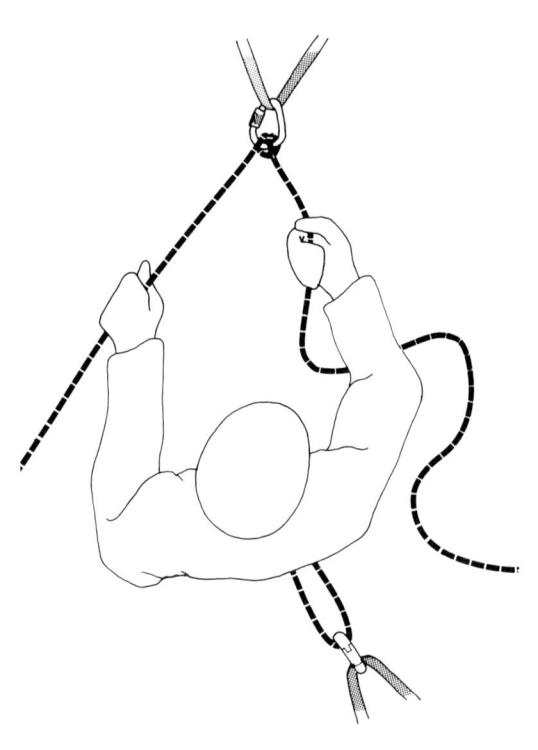

Fig 117 Direct belay using Italian friction hitch. Note separate belay anchor installed to prevent the belayer from being pulled towards the hitch when holding a fall. Belay brakes must not be used for direct belaying in this way, because of the difficulty of initiating the braking action.

Some Special Topics

hand coils the two climbers move simultaneously, flicking the rope which lies between them over and around spikes as they go. The technique can be particularly effective when moving along an exposed but technically simple ridge crest.

CLIMBING SOLO *(Fig 119)*

Common sense tells us never to climb alone, but for those who take delight in solitary mind games and have the experience to cope with unexpected difficulties there is no more exotic setting for the contest than the vertical arena of a rock face. A confident solo climber can feast on a thousand metres of rock while a roped party nibbles on a hundred.

Few climbers are prepared to solo even within three full grades of their top leading standard, and will usually select routes much easier than that. Besides having no conscious desire to commit suicide, there is no room in soloing for the grading snobbery which commonly afflicts roped climbing. The experience is everything.

Protection Techniques *(Fig 120)*

Not everyone solos for the thrill and freedom of climbing unroped. There may be sound practical reasons why you

Fig 118   Climbers moving together along an easy ridge.

Techniques

Fig 119 Soloing an easy climb in the Ogwen Valley.

choose to climb alone, such as when your free time falls mid-week. There are ways of protecting a solo climb on these occasions, although none are entirely satisfactory.

By far the safest method is to hang a fixed rope down the crag and then protect yourself as you climb by sliding a prusik device up the rope. Clearly the method is only suitable for one-pitch routes. Prusik loops are wholly unsuitable for this purpose, and even a mechanical device may fail under the shock load of holding your fall. One solution is to fix the prusik device in such a way that it slides automatically up the rope as you climb. If the route follows a zigzag line you can minimise the risk of a pendulum fall by first abseiling down the fixed rope to place runners at the turning points.

Protecting a multi-pitch route is more complicated and much less secure. First secure one end of the rope to several good anchors (which must be capable of withstanding an upward pull). Now tie a figure-of-eight knot a few metres from this end and clip it to your harness by a locking karabiner. With this dubious protection (if you fall off the force on both you and the anchors will be enormous) you can now set about climbing the pitch, clipping the rope into protection as you go. When the rope threatens to come tight behind you, gather up

Some Special Topics

some slack, tie a knot, and clip this into your harness by a second locking karabiner. Releasing the first knot now frees you to climb another few metres. Repeat the process and eventually you will gain the top of the pitch. Now fix the rope to a new set of anchors and abseil back down the pitch, collecting runners as you go. After removing the lower set of anchors, prusik back up the rope (mechanical devices for speed) to regain the upper ledge. Provided you still have the energy and inclination, you may now repeat the entire procedure on the next pitch.

A faster but less secure method is to climb unroped, protecting the occasional difficult move by clipping a sling into a runner you have placed nearby, which you will hope to flick out before climbing too high! However, since no part of the system is able to absorb energy, even a tiny fall could generate sufficient force to cause the anchor to fail. The practical value of this method, therefore, is in having a nearby sling to grab if things suddenly start to go badly wrong. Will the runner hold? Who knows – soloing can never be considered safe. Each bad mistake rubs out a life.

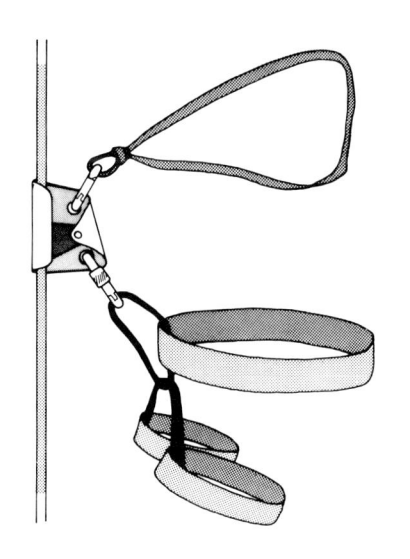

Fig 120   Using a top rope and Clog ascender to protect a solo climb. The lower locking karabiner clips directly into the harness anchor/belaying loop, whereas the upper ordinary karabiner clips into a tape sling worn across the chest like a bandoleer. This chest link pulls the ascender up the rope as you climb, whereas the harness link supports your weight if you fall.

ROCK CLIMBING IN BRITAIN

Fig 121   Powder Monkey Parade, Birchens Edge.

13 A Brief History

Mountaineers were climbing rock for several decades before the period generally identified as the dawn of rock climbing. In the context of mid-nineteenth century Alpine mountaineering – a golden age culminating in Whymper's ascent of the Matterhorn – rock barriers were seen as obstacles to be overcome *en route* to the summit, not as problems worthy of independent attention.

That soon changed. It became fashionable among one group of Alpinists to spend their Christmas and Easter vacations among the temporarily snow-covered British hills. These convenient miniatures of beloved peaks in France and Switzerland, the theory went, would provide useful practice with rope and ice-axe while awaiting the next Alpine summer season. Besides, the stimulating company and festive atmosphere would compensate for the lack of altitude and the mediocrity of the climbing.

During mild winters the Alpinists would encounter not glistening snowfields on Welsh and Lake District mountains but rock ridges and boulder choked gullies. Those battles were won not with the rhythmic swing of the axe but the clawing of fingers and the skittering of boot nails. Later it occurred to some free-thinking enthusiasts to make visits in high summer, when the rocks would be drier and less cold, and there would be much less interference from lingering snow patches.

Mountain historians disagree when asked to single out the climb and climber responsible for initiating the sport of rock climbing as we know it today. Most would nominate Haskett-Smith's solo ascent in the Lake District of the Napes Needle on Great Gable (1886); others would remind us of Puttrell's first steps on Derbyshire gritstone at Wharncliffe Edge (1885); or yet again of Stocker and Wall's climb in Wales on the West Buttress of Lliwedd (1883). The point of origin is less important to us now than the period of consolidation which followed. These were the years of Raeburn in Scotland, O.G. Jones and the Abraham brothers in the Lake District, Archer Thomson in Wales, and Puttrell and Bishop in the Peak District. In them we recognise the spirit of rock climbing which, despite periodic abuse, survives to guide us to this day. Then, as now, climbing was not about getting to the top at all costs but about exploring steep places. Traditions forged one hundred years ago have successfully held at bay a technology which, given free rein, would have destroyed the sport overnight.

Climbs pioneered around the beginning of the twentieth century are among the most popular today. Apart from a few notorious examples their frequent holds are comfortingly large and their ledges spacious – ideal settings for beginners making discoveries about rock and themselves. Amphitheatre Buttress, Grooved Arete, Moss Ghyll, 'C' Ordinary, Black Hawk Slit – these early classics have lost none of their charm with the passage of time.

The sport developed more slowly through the 1920s, having been robbed of several of its leading practitioners by the Great War. A gathering momentum eventually erupted in the 1930s with the emergence of new talent and a new standard of difficulty. The flurry of bold first ascents made on Scafell, Clogwyn du'r Arddu and other major cliffs by Kirkus, Edwards, Linnell, Hargreaves, MacPhee and others, spearheaded a broader if less ambitious thrust towards the mountains by the general public. Never again would rock climbing be the preserve of professional men. The great climbs of the 1930s have become the classic climbs of today. Protected by superior equipment, these are the routes which most beginners aspire to lead within their first year or so of climbing.

It will be instructive to view these achievements in the context of European climbing. The 1930s were notable years for the success and tragedy on the great Alpine north faces of the Matterhorn, Drus, Grandes Jorasses, and Eiger – climbs ten times bigger and far more serious than anything being tackled in Britain. Actual technical difficulties encountered by Cassin or Heckmair would have been a little less severe than those solved by Kirkus or Edwards, but on their climbs they had also to contend with ice, stonefall, storms and debilitating bivouacs. In terms of mountaineering achievement the British were twenty years behind Continental climbers.

If during the 1930s Britain's snowless little mountains produced few top Alpinists, it was only because their flanking crags were busy nurturing skilful rock climbers. Whereas the remaining unclimbed Alpine lines were increasingly being overcome with the aid of pitons (and later, bolts), the British pioneers resisted this tempting but short-sighted solution and instead grew yet more cunning in their 'free climbing' style. Behind them the body of ordinary climbers, by now informally organised into clubs or long running partnerships, followed their example and confirmed the aid-free ethic. Ironically the latest force in Alpinism has elevated free climbing to its highest form of expression on the walls and overhangs which once sprouted the lad-

Fig 122   The Flake Crack of Scafell's Central Buttress. First ascended in 1914 by Herford and Sansom, this most famous of Lake District climbs was fifteen years ahead of its time.

ders of pitons and bolts.

Climbing recovered quickly from the Second World War. Despite petrol rationing and the materialistic aspirations of post-war society, many found the time and motivation to escape each Sunday to the hills and crags. History records the famous climbs of the 1950s (Cenotaph Corner is of this vintage) pioneered by a formidable force represented by such powerful climbers as Cunningham, Smith, Dolphin, Brown and Whillans.

Many of their climbs followed the vertical crack and corner lines which twenty years before had thwarted the best efforts of Kirkus and his contemporaries. Today these routes seem barely more difficult to lead than some of the top routes of 1930s' vintage; yet at the time of their first ascent, routes such as Kipling Groove, Vember and Cemetery Gates were regarded as major breakthroughs. The discrepancy is almost entirely due to improvements in equipment. A vertical crack laced with runners will seem a far easier proposition than a bald rib devoid of protection.

Awesome reputations of the post-war test-pieces held the pack at bay until the 1960s, when 'ordinary' climbers first broke the *Extremely Severe* barrier to herald a decade of hard climbing and fast living. The link between mountaineering and rock climbing was further weakened during that period by a growing interest in sea cliffs and in the limestone outcrops of Avon, Yorkshire and the Peak District. Smooth soled rock boots became generally available and, coupled with better protection equipment and an 'anything goes' attitude, began dismantling what remained of the mental barriers. The *Very Severe* grade came within reach of the majority of enthusiasts, while those of greater skill or ambition would soon find themselves working through the '*Brown Extremes*', which not many years before had been the preserve of Joe Brown and his contemporaries in the legendary Rock and Ice Club.

The early 1970s were bleak years in

Fig 123   The author on Suicide Wall, Cwm Idwal. Climbed by Chris Preston in 1945, after several failed attempts (including those of Kirkus and Edwards in the thirties), this short but serious climb has retained some of its earlier reputation. Graded E2, and not well protected by modern standards, it still demands respect.

Fig 124   Kipling Groove, Gimmer Crag (Langdale). First climbed in 1948 by Arthur Dolphin; a classic of the post-war period.

terms of important new routes. By then it seemed that most of the worthwhile remaining lines could be subjugated only with the aid of pitons. The soothsayers preached doom and despondency. In its blind rush towards technical achievement, the sport appeared to have gone down a blind alley.

Little of this affected the young climbers then discovering rock climbing for themselves. Before them stretched a long apprenticeship of low standard mountain climbs in Skye or Cwm Idwal before graduation to the magical *Very Severes* of small valley crags in Glencoe, Langdale or the Llanberis Pass. They thought themselves rock climbers, but equally they were becoming mountaineers. In winter they would head north to the ice gullies of Scotland; and in summer, south to the rock and snow of the Alps. However, the very young, without knowing it, were poised for change.

Protection equipment improved steadily throughout the early 1970s until it became possible to ascend most climbs in comparative safety. Inevitably climbers responded by attempting routes of proportionately greater difficulty. In climbing it is the threshold of fear, not technical difficulty, which remains constant. Falling became an accepted part of the sport as young climbers cast aside the traditional apprenticeship and flexed their muscles on yesterday's test-piece.

In the mid-1970s standards of difficulty took a leap forward with Livesey, Fawcett and Proctor; first on the limestone of Yorkshire and Derbyshire, then on the mountain rock of Wales and the Lake District. By this time news spread quickly through the pages of specialised magazines. Media exposure built reputations while simultaneously, if unwittingly, encouraging ordinary climbers to 'have a go' – an attitude which persists to this day.

This new impetus coincided with a nationwide fitness boom. Ambitious climbers stopped boozing and started training. The word got around. Within months it became fashionable to run, pump iron, and work out on the indoor climbing walls which had begun to mushroom into existence across the country. These changes produced dramatic results. Livesey's Right Wall in the Llanberis Pass, the first ascent of which had so astounded climbers in 1974,

A Brief History

had by 1984 become a set piece for able climbers seeking an entry into the world of modern wall climbing.

The surge in standards had not been entirely due to training. British climbers touring the United States at this time had followed local practice and used gymnastic chalk to improve hand grip. The benefits were immediate and obvious. Chalk came back with them and like a plague it spread across the country. Cries of outrage from the Establishment were smothered in a cloud of white dust. By the following summer the tell-tale white streaks disfigured rock on the tiniest lowland outcrop and the biggest mountain crag.

High friction rock boots arrived from Spain shortly afterwards. They left no mark and were accepted immediately and without rancour. The benefits of these 'sticky' soles were most evident on harder climbs but, as happened with chalk, climbers operating in the middle grades would not be denied the means of optimising their abilities. Within two years almost all new rock boots sold were fitted with this type of butyl rubber.

The gap widened between those who embraced new attitudes and equipment

Fig 125 On the roof of Sloth, Staffordshire Roaches: a milestone in any leader's roof-climbing career. First climbed in 1952 by Don Whillans and Joe Brown.

Fig 126 Starting the top pitch of Cemetery Gates on Dinas Cromlech; another audacious Brown/Whillans route of the early 1950s.

Rock Climbing in Britain

Fig 127 Debauchery, Matlock High Tor. Along with other limestone classics of the mid-1960s, this route revealed the true free climbing potential of Derbyshire limestone.

and those who could not – or would not – capitulate. Whereas in the 1970s a keen but otherwise unexceptional climber could attempt routes within one or two grades of the hardest, in the 1980s this became a realistic hope only for those of considerable natural ability or willingness to adopt a rigorous training regime.

These new trends had already swept across Europe, the United States and Australia. Young climbers travelling to the Continent now based themselves in Verdon, not Chamonix. Limestone gorges had more to offer than granite mountains. Nevertheless it would be a mistake to suppose that rock climbing and mountaineering are now mutually exclusive. Today there are still mountaineers who maintain a high level of proficiency on rock while developing their interest in winter climbing, Alpinism and Himalayan mountaineering.

Perhaps we are too ready to assume that the sport always takes its direction from the front line. There is evidence to the contrary; for instance the thumbs-down verdict passed by the central core of climbers on elaborate aid climbs of the 1960s (after a brief period of notoriety most of these fell into disuse). Out of that dissatisfaction grew the dynamic 'all free' trend of the 1970s. It is ironic that this movement is itself turning sour because of dubious practices (resting on the rope, deliberate falling, top roping, pre-placing of protection) which collectively constitute what we might refer to as 'ascent by attrition'. Doubtless the rank and file will offer up their verdict on this style of climbing in due course!

14 British Crags and Climbs

Britain lacks truly dramatic mountain scenery. Nothing here can compare with the granite domes of Yosemite Valley or the toothed spires of the Dolomites. Instead we have green hills dotted with little crags that barely warrant a second glance from sightseers. Size, however, is not the only measure of worth in climbs of quality. Study the guidebooks and you will see that in fact we have thousands of fine climbs among our hills and coastlines, some of which have become world famous. A lifetime of regular climbing could never exhaust even half these possibilities.

Most climbs are short – less than a hundred metres – and therefore purity of line and delight in movement are held in high regard. Some of our best routes are found on gritstone outcrops no more than ten metres high. Nevertheless we can also boast some fine mountain climbs set among rugged scenery. Much of the pleasure in these climbs depends not so much on individual moves as on the elevated situations.

What follows is a brief summary of the location and special character of favourite British climbing grounds.

SCOTLAND

Scottish mountain crags are generally bigger and more remote than those of the Lake District and Wales, and as they are situated further from population centres are climbed that much less often. In poor weather the big cliffs suffer badly from their altitude and northern aspect, drying slowly after prolonged rain. In recompense the experience of climbing here during fine weather can be almost Alpine in character.

Two other factors conspire to ruin Scottish rock climbing holidays – snow and midges. In England and Wales snow rarely arrives before December or survives beyond April; in Scotland the winter season often extends from November through to May, with snow patches on the high crags lingering into June or early July. Midges work the summer shift, doing overtime in July and August to help cope with the influx of tourists. Depending on the area, a visit arranged in May, June or September will avoid the worst of both scourges.

(a) Northern Highlands

Sea stacks of the far north (Old Man of Hoy, Old Man of Stoer), and the huge overhanging prow of Strone Ulladale on Harris, continue to inspire pilgrimages despite formidable logistical problems both on and off the routes. Further south the remote Carnmore area boasts several long climbs, some over 300m, at all standards and on good rock. Carnmore Crag itself has some impressive climbs in the higher grades.

Rock Climbing in Britain

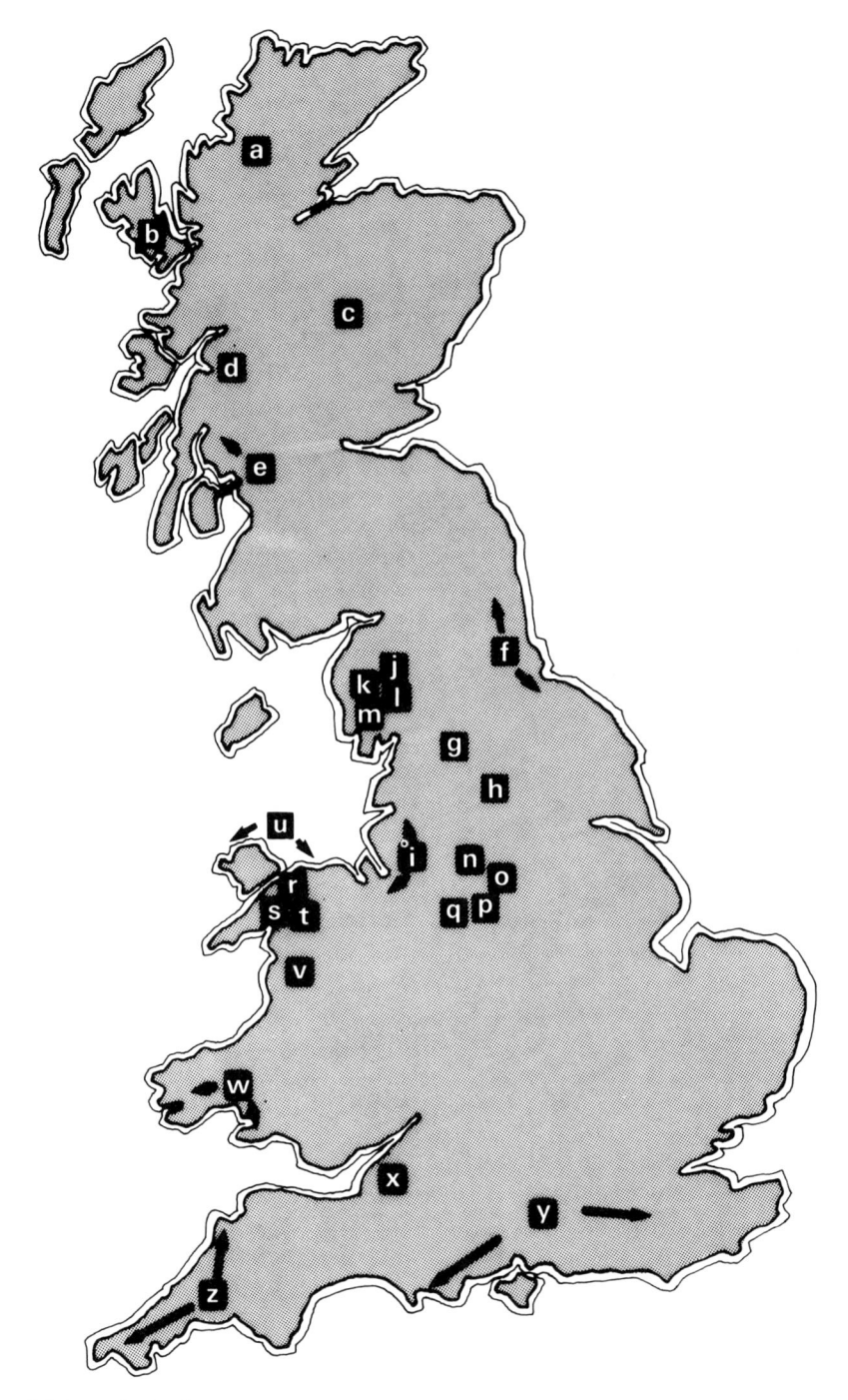

Fig 128 Main rock climbing areas in Britain (letters refer to those in the text).

(b) Skye

The Black Cuillin of Skye are without doubt the best loved of Scottish rock peaks. Most climbs take advantage of the rough gabbro rock and so warrant the lower and middle classifications of difficulty. The best known ascend the 300m high north-west face of Sron na Ciche from which protrudes the distinctive and much photographed Cioch. The twelve-hour traverse of the Cuillin Ridge receives widespread acclaim as one of the best mountaineering expeditions in Britain.

(c) Cairngorms

Much of the best climbing takes place on large crags which flank the remote Cairngorm peaks. Some of the hardest are found on the forbidding walls of Shelter Stone Crag; those on Coire Etchachan will seem a little more welcoming. Climbs at Lochnagar – south-east of the main Cairngorm group – receive most attention from winter climbers, unlike the 300m high routes of quality which find devious ways up the extensive Craig an Dubh-loch on Broad Cairn. Both cliffs are many hours from the nearest road.

(d) Glencoe

First time visitors to Scotland invariably make for Glencoe and its wealth of accessible climbing. Routes of all standards (lengths 75–100m) await on crags lining the south side of the glen: Buachaille Etive Mor, east face of Gearr Aonach, east and west faces of Aonach Dubh. Some miles further south the 200m Etive Slabs pose quite different problems with their friction climbs on granite set at a deceptively gentle angle.

Ben Nevis is best known for its magnificent winter climbing, and yet in summer the buttresses defining the corries of its north side entertain with rock climbs of most standards of difficulty and lengths of 300m or more. Some harder climbs weave impressive lines up the chiselled features of Carn Dearg, a huge cliff which dominates the approach.

(e) Southern Regions

Good climbing in Scotland is not confined to the far north. That on The Cobbler (Arrochar region) lies within reasonable daily travelling distance of Glasgow. For those who prefer the island atmosphere, the enchanting Isle of Arran offers excellent climbing in the middle grades. Much of this will be found on Cir Mhor, a sharp peak of coarse grained granite which rises from the head of Glen Rosa.

NORTHERN ENGLAND

Some outcrops enjoy a popularity out of all proportion to their apparent worth, as if proximity to a large town is reason enough. Although many of the northern outcrops fall into this category, a number have national significance.

Three types of crag will be encountered: natural outcrops of gritstone or sandstone sitting in small piles at the edge of bleak moorland; limestone scars and gorges interrupting the pretty scenery of bubbling dales; and disused quarries of either rock type burrowing into the back yard of the towns they once supplied.

Rock Climbing in Britain

Fig 129 Eastern Buttress, Sron na Ciche.

(f) Northumberland and North York Moors

Outcrops of good quality, coarse sandstone maintain a faithful clientele from the industrial towns of the north-east – Middlesborough, Durham, Newcastle. Further north, the Cheviots have longer climbs on volcanic rock.

(g) Yorkshire Limestone

Limestone cliffs at Malham, Gordale and Kilnsey – at one time the preserve of aid climbers – have become forcing grounds for free climbers. The continuously overhanging central wall at Malham is almost 100m high. The wings are shorter and less steep but also catch the winter sun. Climbs deep within the gorge at Gordale fail to shake off their dismal surroundings at any time of year. Climbs at Kilnsey overhang alarmingly; almost all are in the highest grades, while spectacular aid climbs breach a 10m roof set high on the South Buttress. Smaller limestone scars at Attermire, Twistleton and Great Close have some excellent climbs set at a more amenable angle.

(h) Yorkshire Gritstone

A reputation for brutal crack climbing and dismal scenery is not wholly deserved by the grit outcrops of Yorkshire. The delightfully situated Brimham Rocks have slabby walls in addition to the aforesaid brutal cracks, plus numerous free-standing pinnacles (the ascent of which baffle climbers and tourists alike). A large quarry adds to the variety at Ilkley, which otherwise consists of several small outcrops of sound gritstone. Almscliff enjoys a fanatical local following, but repels the best efforts of outsiders on its 10m walls. Other outcrops are of limited interest, although each has its unique character. Widdop has a large and intriguing buttress climbable at a low standard, while Eastby has some unusual 20m slab climbs.

(i) Lancashire and Cheshire

Grit quarries of South Lancashire are unable to escape their industrial origins. The outlook from most of them is depressing. The compensation is technically interesting and often quite serious climbing. Not all quarries are dismal and difficult, but only local climbers will spare the time to seek them out. In Cheshire the natural sandstone outcrop at Helbsy commands a prettier view than most thereabouts – the oil refinery of Ellesmere Port.

LAKE DISTRICT

Lake District crags have lost none of their appeal in the hundred years since they were first explored by rock climbers. The sea cliffs and lowland outcrops of Wales will be sadly missed during cold weather, but in summer the mountain crags lack nothing in atmosphere and quality of climbing. The scenery is enchanting.

When dry the lichenous rock of mountain crags provides excellent foot friction, but when wet (which it frequently is) it can be lethally slippery. South facing valley crags dry more quickly after rain. These low level climbs are typically 50–75m in length, while those nearer the summits may be 150m or longer.

The major valleys radiate outwards

from a central massif of high fells. Travel from one valley to another frequently involves a long detour by road, or alternatively a two-hour walk over a high pass. For this reason it is common practice to spend a few days climbing from a single valley base.

(j) Borrowdale

Some of the low lying valley crags dry quickly after wet weather (Shepherd's) but not others (Goat Crag). A number of the big Wasdale crags may be approached from here by a long walk, adding to the options.

Fig 130   Scafell Crag.

(k) Wasdale

In good weather this is much the best base, as several of the most important mountain crags are approached from here. Scafell Crag has several absorbing climbs in the lower and middle grades, in addition to the famous and difficult Central Buttress. Scafell's East Buttress generally sets harder challenges. Esk Buttress, romantically situated at the head of Eskdale, offers good climbing only in the middle and upper grades.

The Napes sit high on Great Gable facing the sun. Most routes are in the lower grades, including the Needle Ridge with its optional and historic Needle. Pillar Rock deters many with the prospect of a long approach, but this huge obelisk rewards those making the pilgrimage with situations as impressive as any in the country.

(l) Langdale

This delightful valley is a particular favourite among those arriving from the south. Inevitably it becomes very crowded during summer weekends, but climbs of all grades on a variety of high mountain faces and south facing valley crags guarantee its continuing popularity. Gimmer Crag, the best of them, can claim several classics in the middle and higher grades – all on excellent rock.

(m) Dow Crag

A long climb on Dow (100m or more) makes an excellent introduction to Lake District climbing. Harder problems add spice to subsequent visits. Its firm, rough rock provides superb friction in dry

Fig 131   Krypton Route, Mystery Buttress, Widdop.

weather, but becomes extremely slippery when wet. A secluded setting above Goat's Water adds to the overall appeal.

PEAK DISTRICT

Gritstone edges of the Peak continue to play a major part in introducing new climbers to the sport. Most crags face west, catching the afternoon sun and drying quickly after rain. The rock, invariably rough and reliable, responds best to a confident and dynamic approach. Though often as short as 10m, many of these climbs are as memorable as any.

As in Yorkshire, the limestone outcrops present quite different challenges. Most rise from tree-lined river valleys; pleasant in spring and autumn, but steamy in summer and slow to dry in winter. Universally steep and intimidating, few climbs on these 20–50m walls will appeal to beginners.

(n) Northern Edges

These sombre edges are much less popular than sunnier outcrops further east. However, they are convenient for those travelling from Manchester and the west. Some outcrops appeal mainly to beginners (Windgather, Castle Naze), others to the more experienced (Shining Clough, Wimberry). The remote Kinder edges include routes of most standards but are largely neglected.

Fig 132   Whit's End Direct, Gimmer Crag.

Fig 133   Tarkus, Dow Crag.

(o) Quarries

Inferior climbing and outlook characterise most quarried edges, but one of them – Millstone Edge – has many excellent climbs of 20–35m length. Most of these are in the higher grades. The rounded ledges and bulging fissures typical of natural edges are absent here, replaced by flat holds and clean cut cracks.

(o) Eastern Edges

The best gritstone climbing is to be found among the edges which line the moors south-west of Sheffield. Despite their exposed setting, most face west and will dry quickly after rain. Stanage is the best known and most popular of them. It has hundreds of excellent climbs at all standards, some quite long for gritstone (20m). Tall bays at the southern end are frequently crowded, but the edge is four miles long so there are plenty of quiet corners! Though less extensive, Froggatt and Curbar contain routes of similar quality. Routes at Curbar tend to be steep and intimidating, whereas Froggatt adds slab climbs and a difficult pinnacle to the usual crack and wall climbs.

(p) Limestone

Impressive limestone prows in Chee Dale give steep climbing in the higher grades. Several routes here have attained classic status. Stony Middleton continues to focus limestone aspirations, despite its grubby setting. Most good climbs are difficult, a number of them tackling the 30m high Windy Ledge Buttress. The picturesque Dovedale and Manifold valleys boast excellent conventional climbs on 40m walls (Ravenstor, Beeston Tor) as well as some unusual free and aid routes based on strange rock formations (Dove Holes, Ilam Rock, Thor's Cave). Set high above Matlock, the imposing 50m face of High Tor concentrates a number of modern classics in the higher grades.

(p) Southern Edges

Southern grit edges typically comprise isolated buttresses set among pleasant woods or moorland. Birchens is especially popular, not least because most good climbs are in the lower grades and are not too steep. Imposing prows at Cromford Black Rocks give more awkward problems on bulging rock. Similar delights and difficulties await at Cratcliffe Tor.

Fig 134   Delicatessen, High Tor.

Fig 135 Valkyrie, Roaches Lower Tier.

(q) Staffordshire Grit

The longest gritstone climbs (30m) will be found at the Roaches – a fascinating collection of towers set high on the moors between Buxton and Leek. The rocks are particularly convenient for climbers travelling from the west and south. Dozens of compelling routes of all styles and standards await. Castle-like walls of nearby Hen Cloud and the prows of Ramshaw Rocks add to the variety.

NORTH WALES

No other region in Britain can offer climbing of such variety as the mountains and sea cliffs of Wales. Rock varies from the white limestone of the north coast to the dark volcanic rock of central Snowdonia. Much of this is of good quality, although on average the rock is more friable than is usual in the Lake District. The footholds on many of the popular routes in traditional areas have become rounded and slippery with continuous use – a process begun a hundred years ago by the nailed boots of the pioneers.

Approaches are generally shorter than in Scotland or the Lake District; an hour's walk will get you to most crags. Travel between groups is also easier. For these reasons the choice of base is not so critical, although most climbers continue to gather in Llanberis or Ogwen.

(r) Ogwen Area

This is probably the best centre for beginners, although it lacks poor weather alternatives. Popular 120m slabs at Idwal look easy but prove to be serious outings at their grade. Walls set into the slabs give harder climbing of equal seriousness on rough, pocketed rock – the infamous Suicide Wall among them. The distinctive peak of Tryfan has easy but energetic climbs on its Milestone Buttress, and some delightful 200m mountaineering routes on its East Face. Nearby Glyder Fach is steeper and has some excellent crack and groove climbs. Crags found lurking among the Carneddau hills on the opposite side of the valley are equally worthwhile though less popular. Craig yr Ysfa is the best of them. Wonderfully remote, its 250m Amphitheatre Buttress is a *VDiff* classic.

Fig 136   Mur y Niwl, Craig yr Ysfa.

(s) Llanberis Pass

The popular 'Three Cliffs' rise above scree slopes just fifteen minutes from the road. Dinas Cromlech, the best of them, has several 50m wall, crack and corner climbs on vertical rock. Cenotaph Corner, centre-piece of the crag, is the most famous climb in Britain. In the shadows opposite lurks Dinas Mot, regarded by many as the most interesting cliff in the valley. Precarious friction moves on the Nose contrast with energetic roof climbing through the eaves of the Wings. Another 20 minutes' walking brings Cyrn Las within reach. The long (150m) and serious Main Wall here is one of the best *Severes* in Britain, and its near neighbour The Grooves one of the best *Extremes*. Beyond lay the hidden delights of remote Clogwyn y Ddysgl.

(s) Snowdon Group

Lliwedd and its 300m high buttresses held the undivided attention of the country's best climbers at the beginning of the nineteenth century. It now languishes in almost total neglect. The potential for unwatched adventure is unlimited. Clogwyn du'r Arddu ('Cloggy') held a similar position in the 1930s but weathered fads and fashions with more success. It remains one of the most important cliffs in Britain. All worthwhile climbs are *Very Severe* or harder: intimidating walls and cracks on the East Buttress, serious 150-200m slabs on the West.

(t) Tremadog and Moelwyns

The coastal cliffs at Tremadog receive less than a third of the rainfall suffered by inland crags. The rock is a delight to climb and there are many fine routes in the higher grades. Some of the best will be found on the imposing 60m Vector Buttress. A handful of excellent routes at *Severe* standard adds to the other amenities – short approaches, car-park and convenient café. The Moelwyn crags are nearer the mountains (and rain). These 50–100m routes on pocketed rock would have become extremely popular but for their location, and are an ideal venue for comparative beginners.

(u) Sea Cliffs

The Great Orme on the North Wales coast has many top quality limestone climbs. Long, serious routes on the forbidding Little Orme are less popular. The pleasant inland crag of Craig y Forwyn has more appeal for the middle grade climber. Unfortunately the crag suffers from chronic access problems.

Sea cliffs of 100m at Gogarth on Anglesey reward the competent with impressive and occasionally frightening situations. Most good climbs are difficult (*Hard Very Severe* or harder). Although much of the rock is excellent, some of the best routes, paradoxically, climb rock of dreadful quality. Routes on Castell Helen and the Upper Tier are the best introductions, while those on the Main Cliff and Wen Zawn are better saved until you have the measure of the place.

(v) Mid Wales

Mountain crags on Cader Idris (Cyfrwy) and the Arans (Craig Cywarch, Gist Ddu) are little visited. Although much of the rock is loose or vegetated, some

Fig 137   Void, Tremadog.

memorable days await the discerning climber.

SOUTH AND SOUTH WEST

An absence of mountains need not imply a lack of good rock climbs. This is the case in the south-west of England and Wales, where the coastlines of Pembroke, Devon and Cornwall contain a tremendous number of fine climbs on limestone, shale and granite. Major inland crags near Bristol and on Dartmoor add to the area's potential. By comparison the south-east of England is poorly served. Leaving aside the esoteric chalk cliffs on the south coast, only the small sandstone outcrops of Kent give worthwhile climbing. Nevertheless these miniature climbs pose some intriguing problems.

The weather tends to be milder here than anywhere else in Britain. It is usually possible to climb throughout the winter months. Those with private transport and a couple of weeks to spare could devise a fascinating tour taking in the whole south-western region. Otherwise, West Cornwall has the most to offer those wishing to climb routes in the lower and middle grades from a fixed base.

(w) South-west Wales

The rugged Pembrokeshire coastline contains many fine limestone climbs of 30–50m height and in the upper grades. Good rock and comforting holds take the sting out of unremitting verticality. St David's Head also has some low standard climbs on granite. Sea cliffs of the Gower peninsula include an unusually large proportion of easy climbs. The rock is limestone; rough and firm at sea-level, but tending towards looseness on the upper cliffs.

(x) Bristol Area

Limestone walls of 50–80m height in the Avon Gorge provide many exciting climbs, although at times their popularity and proximity to a main road detracts. Spectacular climbs in the Cheddar Gorge are subject to a ban from Easter to October (the tourist season) because of the danger from falling rocks.

Rock Climbing in Britain

Fig 138   Zawn Face Route, Land's End.

(y) South-east and South Coast

Sandstone outcrops in Kent enjoy a popularity out of all proportion to their scope and height (5–10m). The best climbing is at Harrison's Rocks, where top ropes are frequently employed to combat the soft rock. Huge, crumbling chalk cliffs at Dover have been climbed using ice-axes and crampons – a practice few will wish to emulate. Limestone cliffs at Swanage and Berry Head are climbed using more conventional techniques. Access to some routes is complicated by tides or seasonal bans imposed for the protection of nesting birds.

(z) Devon and Cornwall

Inland tors on Dartmoor, including the Dewerstone, give climbs of 30–50m on sound granite. The north coasts of Devon and Cornwall are noted for serious climbs on big sea cliffs of indifferent rock (Tintagel Head, Pentire Head, Carn Gowla) plus some more amenable slab climbs on better rock at Baggy Point. Superb granite climbs in the middle and high grades on Lundy include the famous 125m Devil's Slide. Accommodation on the island is restricted and visits must be booked. Many of the best and most popular climbs in the lower and middle grades are concentrated in West Cornwall at Bosigran and Chair Ladder. The rock here is firm granite and up to 60m high.

APPENDIX

Fig 139   Abseiling down the right wall of Cenotaph Corner.

Grading Systems

Originators of rock climbs allocate grades to their routes on a scale ranging from *Easy* to *Extremely Severe*. These are later confirmed or modified by the guide writer. The grade of a route is the single most important piece of information to those who wish to repeat the ascent. In time climbers get a feel for what grade of route lies within their ability, although naturally this will be modified according to weather conditions, current level of fitness, type of climbing and so on.

The need to differentiate between safe and serious routes has brought about a dual grading system. In this the adjectival component assesses the overall proposition, while the numerical component attempts to assess pure technical difficulty. Aid climbs have a grading system of their own, based on a combined assessment of seriousness and ease of aid placement (since the two are often closely related).

Despite sharing a common system, in Britain it is rarely possible to make direct grade comparisons between the regions. Although first encounters with unfamiliar rock are always disconcerting, major discrepancies remain and so it is wise to approach a new area with caution.

Comparisons between neighbouring routes can be equally misleading. Some climbers excel on strenuous cracks, others on delicate slabs. The guide writer can only attempt to steer a compromising line. The final responsibility – as always – rests with the climber.

Other countries have developed grading systems of their own. Grades in the United States and Australia are entirely numerical, whereas those allocated to climbs in the Western Alps have both overall and technical components. Some European countries grade their outcrop climbs on a separate scale, adding to the confusion. The UIAA have tried to convert everyone to their international system of numerical grades, but with only mixed success. At present it is used primarily for mountain rock climbs in the Eastern Alps and for pitch grading in the Western Alps.

THE BRITISH GRADING SYSTEM

These adjectival grades and their standard abbreviations indicate overall difficulty (note that their literal meanings have been lost to antiquity).

Easy (E) Mainly scrambling, although a rope may be used to protect exposed sections. Not generally regarded as proper rock climbing.
Moderate (M) Rock climbing in the true sense of the word, but with large holds on rock set at a comfortable angle. A single rope plus small selection of slings and nuts will suffice.
Difficult (D) Entertaining climbing on good holds. Suitable for beginners and for first leads, although the angle may occasionally approach vertical.
Very Difficult (VDiff) Climbing of a more sustained nature, demanding a

Appendix

thoughtful and enthusiastic approach if beginners are to succeed. There are many good climbs at this standard. Rock boots could be an advantage, and a broad selection of runners will be required.

Severe (S) Steep, sustained climbing on good holds, or perhaps slab climbing with some poor holds. Complete beginners generally find these routes too demanding.

Very Severe (VS) Sustained climbing encompassing all kinds of features and techniques, probably with several baffling moves. An enthusiastic beginner could be climbing these routes within a year. There are many famous routes at this grade. Rock boots and a comprehensive set of runners will be required.

Hard Very Severe (HVS) These are advanced routes, demanding a determined approach coupled with cunning and experience. Double ropes, micro-wires and camming devices could prove useful.

Extremely Severe (E1, 2, 3, etc.) This is the top grade, now split into several categories. Most enthusiasts will aspire to climb the famous E1 and E2 routes, and in time will probably succeed. E3 and E4 routes are either exceptionally serious or technically very demanding. Routes graded E5 and upwards represent the most difficult and/or serious routes in the country.

The numerical grade indicates the maximum technical difficulty that will be encountered on the pitch. The system is unbounded, allowing for future increases in standard. At present it extends from 1 to 7. Each category is further subdivided by adding the letter a, b or c. Technical grades are not readily applied to the easier routes and so those in common use are: 4a, 4b, 4c, 5a, 5b, 5c, 6a, 6b, 6c, 7a. A complete beginner should be able to solve 4a moves, whereas relatively few climbers will ever develop the finger strength or technique to lead those rated 6b or harder.

The crux pitch of a typical *VS* climb would rate 4c; that of an *HVS*, 5a; and of an *E1*, 5b. Using those as the yardstick, an unusual combination of overall and technical grade will reveal something special about the climbing. For instance the crux moves on a route graded *VS 5a* will be very well protected, whereas those on an *E1 5a* will not be. The implication being that a *VS* leader will only attempt 5a moves in a safe situation, whereas an *Extreme* leader will expect to deal with moves of that difficulty regardless of the seriousness.

Aid Routes

Aid routes are given wholly numerical grades:

A0 Occasional aid moves on mostly free routes.

A1 Continuous but straightforward aid climbing.

A2 Routes with some awkward reaches or suspect placements, or severely overhanging routes climbed on reliable *in situ* placements.

A3 Serious routes with several awkward placements or reaches on overhanging and/or suspect rock.

A4 Serious routes of all types, involving many marginal placements – perhaps including *rurps* or *skyhooks* – and with long fall potential.

INTERNATIONAL GRADING COMPARISONS

No direct comparison exists between systems, so the relationships implied here are very approximate. The systems are unbounded and presently extend to E9, 7b, X and 5.13. Only the most commonly compared grades are given here.

UK	UK (technical)	UIAA	US
D		III−, III	
VD		III+, IV−	
S		IV, IV+, V−	
VS	(4b), 4c, (5a)	V−, V, V+, VI−	5.6, 5.7, 5.8
HVS	(4c), 5a, (5b)	VI	5.9
E1	(5a), 5b, (5c)	VI+, VII−	5.10a, 5.10b
E2	(5b), 5c		5.10c, 5.10d
E3	(5c), 6a		5.11a, 5.11b

Glossary

Not all terms listed here appear in the main text; they are included as an aid to deciphering guidebooks and magazine articles.

The glossary assumes an understanding of the following five common terms:

1. **Anchor** General term for a temporary or permanent fixing point for the rope.
2. **Crack** Any fissure in the rock varying in width from less than a millimetre to a few tens of centimetres.
3. **Hold** Any small rock feature used by the hands or feet for balance or support.
4. **A move** Movement from one set of holds to the next.
5. **Route** Course taken by a climb.

ABMG Association of British Mountain Guides (qualified professional instructors).
Abseil Method of descending by sliding down a fixed rope.
Accessory cord Rope of between 4mm and 8mm diameter.
Aid point Anchor used as a hand or foothold.
Aid route Route climbed by pulling up on anchors instead of natural holds.
Amphitheatre Large recess in the cliff face.
Angle peg V-shaped piton placed in wide cracks.
Arete Sharp-edged rock feature similar to the exterior corner of a building.
Artificial Refers to a route which seeks out difficulties despite the proximity of easier climbing. Also an alternative term for aid route.
Ascender Mechanical device for ascending a fixed rope.
Back and foot Method of climbing a chimney by working the back and feet against opposing walls.
Back off Retreat intimidated by the prospect of making a difficult move.
Back rope Method of safeguarding the second on a difficult traverse.
Balance climbing Method of climbing where most of the body weight is supported by footholds, the hands being used merely to maintain balance.
Bandoleer Shoulder sling used to carry equipment.
Belay anchor An anchor which secures the belaying climber.
Belaying Means of handling the rope (usually through a friction device) to safeguard a companion. The term belay is sometimes improperly used for belay anchor.
Belay brake (plate) Friction device used in belaying the rope.
Blind move A move to gain a hidden hold.
Block Protruding lump of rock, possibly detached from the main face.
BMC British Mountaineering Council (governing body of the sport).
Body harness Elaborate harness which ensures that the body is maintained in an upright position after a fall.
Bold Climbing Intimidating climbing which responds best to a confident

143

Glossary

approach.
Bollard Small rock pillar.
Bolt Metal anchor fixed into a hole previously drilled in blank rock, consisting of a threaded sleeve, high tensile bolt, and bolt hanger (eye for karabiner).
Bolt route An aid route climbed using bolts as the means of progress.
Bong V-shaped piton placed in very wide cracks.
Bouldering Unroped climbing on small crags.
Bowline Knot commonly used when tying to the climbing rope.
Bridging Method of ascending V-shaped rock features by working the feet up opposing walls.
Bulge Small overhang.
Buttress Large, definable section of a cliff.
Cairn Small pile of stones erected to mark a path junction, start of a route, mountain summit, etc.
Camming device Anchor consisting of sprung metal cams which expand automatically to fit any width of crack within its expansion range.
Capstone Slab of rock blocking the exit from a chimney.
CC Climbers' Club (major national club with responsibility for producing guidebooks).
Chalk Light magnesium carbonate, in block or powder form, rubbed on to fingers for drying sweat and thereby improving grip on difficult moves (leaves unsightly white marks on the rock unless used in moderation). Carried in a chalk bag slung around waist or clipped to harness.
Cheating Ascending a free climb by unfair means, for example pulling up on runners.

Chest harness Chest support combined with a sit-harness to make a body harness.
Chimney A vertical fissure into which most or all of the body will enter (willingly or otherwise).
Chimneying Method of ascending a chimney by wedging and raising the body using palms, back, knees, feet – anything.
Chock Alternative term for a nut.
Chockstone A rock wedged in a crack.
Classic abseil Basic method of abseiling without harness or friction device.
Classic route Major route widely acclaimed for its quality.
Clean climbing Alternative term for free climbing.
Cleaning Removing lichen, grass, soil, loose rock, etc. from a potential new route prior to the attempt.
Climbing wall Indoor training facility constructed to resemble a rock face.
Clogger Trade name for a popular type of ascender.
Clove hitch Knot sometimes used in securing to a belay anchor
Combined tactics Standing on a companion's back or shoulder to help overcome a holdless start to a climb.
Committing move A move beyond which there is no hope of dignified retreat.
Corner Rock feature similar to the interior corner of a room.
Couloir A broad gully.
Cow's tail Short length of rope clipped between harness and aid point to support body weight.
Crag General term for a cliff face, rock outcrop or quarry.
Cruise Fluent ascent of a difficult route (i.e. no falls or yo-yos).

Crux Most difficult section of a climb.
Cwm (also Coire, Cirque) Large hollow in the mountainside.
Delicate move A precarious move using small holds.
Descender (Descendeur) Mechanical friction device used when abseiling.
Desperate move A very difficult move.
Direct belay Time-saving method of belaying the rope.
Double fisherman's Knot used when joining two ropes.
Dynamic belay The usual method of belaying which allows some rope to slip through the belay device to help absorb fall energy.
EBs Trade name for a once-popular type of rock boot.
Edging Technique of using small footholds by applying the inner edge of the boot sole. Also refers to rock boots particularly suited to this technique.
Escapable Section of climb which is easily quitted for a less demanding alternative.
Etrier Short ladder made from nylon webbing and used as a foot support on aid routes.
Exposed Section of climb where the climber is likely to be aware of the drop below and possibly intimidated by it.
Extension sling (Extender) Loop of rope or tape used to lengthen a runner.
Fall factor An indication of the severity of a fall based on the peak force developed in the system (as opposed to the distance fallen).
F&RCC Fell and Rock Climbing Club (major national club with responsibility for producing guidebooks).
Figure-of-eight Knot with several applications. Also a common type of descender.
Fires (pronounced fee-rays) Trade name for popular type of sticky boot.
Flake Rock feature formed by partial peeling of the surface layer.
Free climbing Climbing a route without resorting to pulling up on runners and so on.
Friable Rock which is liable to crumble when subjected to body weight.
Frictioning up Using the frictional support of boot soles placed flat against the rock as an optimistic means of gaining height in the absence of footholds.
Friend Trade name for the original self-expanding camming device.
Frigging Alternative term for cheating.
Gardening Alternative term for cleaning.
Gear General term for climbing equipment. Also (loosely) an alternative term for protection.
Girdle traverse A route which crosses the cliff from one side to the other, usually at mid-height.
Glacis Gently angled slab.
Grade The difficulty rating allocated to a route.
Granite Type of compact and coarse grained volcanic rock.
Greasy rock Rock made slippery by a coating of damp moss or lichen.
Gripped State of terror induced by difficult climbing and the fear of falling.
Gritstone A compact, coarse grained and generally reliable rock type common in the Pennines.
Groove Rock feature similar to a corner but generally more obtuse (shallow groove) or more acute (V-groove).
Guide Professional climbing instructor. Also a shortened term for guidebook.

Glossary

Gully A trough several metres wide usually extending the full height of the cliff.

Hand traverse A traverse furnished with handholds but no footholds.

Hanging stance A stance where the climber is supported by the belay anchors.

Hawser-laid Nylon climbing rope, now little used, of the open (i.e. sheathless) type of construction.

Heel hook Gymnastic move in which the body is temporarily supported by placing the heel on a hold above the head.

Helmet Lightweight climbing helmet worn as partial protection against falling stones and head-first falls.

Hexentric (Hex) Type of nut of irregular hexagon cross-section.

Incut Small, in-sloping finger hold.

Inescapable Section of climbing not easily quitted for less difficult climbing nearby.

In situ Refers to equipment (usually an anchor) left permanently in place.

Italian friction hitch Sliding knot used as an alternative to the belay brake.

Jamming Method of ascending cracks by wedging the fingers, hands or feet.

Jug Large, secure handhold (derived from jug handle.)

Jumar Trade name for a common type of ascender.

Karabiner Metal clip primarily used as an intermediate link between the climbing rope and a runner.

Kernmantel Nylon climbing rope of core-and-sheath construction.

Kingpin Trade name for common type of piton with medium thickness blade.

Kletterschuhe Rock boot fitted with a stiff, treaded sole.

Knifeblade Type of thin blade piton.

Knife edge Sharp-edged rock feature.

Krab Common shortened version of the term karabiner.

Lasso Thankfully rare means of continuing a climb by throwing a loop of rope over a rock projection and swarming up it.

Layaway move Momentarily laybacking with one hand and foot while reaching for a conventional hold.

Laybacking Method of ascending a crack by leaning back and walking the feet up a holdless wall while gripping the edge of the crack with the hands.

Leader The climber who ascends the pitch first.

Ledge Any flat area on the rock face extending from a few centimetres to a few metres in width.

Leeper Trade name for a Z-shaped angle piton.

Leg loops Component of a sit-harness which supports the thighs.

Limestone Type of fine grained sedimentary rock, usually steep and frequently overhanging, commonly found in the Pennines and on the Welsh coastline.

Line Succession of rock features followed by a route.

Live rope That part of the rope between belayer and climber (as opposed to dead or slack rope which lies in reserve).

Lob off Fall off.

Locking karabiner Type of karabiner fitted with a sleeve to prevent accidental opening.

Lower off Means of regaining the stance after a fall or failure by using the rope to support body weight.

Mantelshelf Small ledge above holdless rock gained in the manner of a swim-

mer emerging from a pool.
Marginal placement A poor runner thought likely to fail if subjected to the force of a long fall.
MIC Mountain Instructor Certificate.
Micro-wire Small wire placed in fine cracks.
Moving together Method of belaying 'on the move' whereby two roped climbers may ascend simultaneously.
Niche Small cave.
Nose Protruding mass of rock.
Nut General term for the metal wedge type of anchor.
Nut key Strip of metal used in removing stubborn nuts.
Off-width Crack which is too wide to be climbed by comfortable jamming.
On sight lead A difficult route climbed without the benefit of prior knowledge gained during abseil inspection or a top roped ascent.
Outcrop A small crag.
Overgraded Refers to a route on which the climbing proves easier than is implied by the grade allocated.
Overhang Rock which bulges out beyond the vertical.
Overlap Small overhang.
PAs Trade name for the original smooth soled rock boot. Now loosely applied to all types of rock boot.
Peel off Fall off.
Pedestal Flat-topped pillar of rock.
Peg Common alternative term for a piton.
Peg hammer Tool used for hammering pitons into cracks.
Pendule Method of swinging across on the rope to gain another line of ascent.
Pinch Type of protruding handhold utilised by gripping the rock between fingers and thumb.

Pinnacle Partially detached pillar of rock.
Pitch Section of route between consecutive stances.
Piton Metal anchor consisting of a blade (which enters the crack) and an eye (into which the karabiner is clipped).
Placement Alternative term for an anchor.
Pocket hold Surface flaw in the rock giving a secure hold.
Polished holds Holds worn smooth by regular use.
Prodder Alternative term for a nut key.
Protection General term for the security offered by runners.
Prow Rock feature similar to a ship's bow.
Prusiking Method of ascending a fixed rope using loops held in place by prusik knots.
Psyche up Prepare mentally for a difficult route.
Psyched out Inability to continue the climb because of excessive nervous anxiety.
Psychological runner A poor anchor placed mainly to boost confidence before attempting a difficult move (i.e. the climber pretends that the runner will hold a fall).
Quartz White, crystalline rock which commonly occurs in bands within other rock types.
Quick-draw Trade name for popular type of extender.
Rack The selection of equipment (nuts etc.) carried up a climb.
Ramp Narrow strip of rock which slants diagonally across the face.
Rappel Alternative term for abseil.
Reverse Climb back down the moves

Glossary

just ascended.
Rib A slender pillar of rock.
Ridge A raised crest, perhaps extending the full height of the cliff.
Rock Trade name for a popular type of wedge-shaped nut.
Roof Large overhang.
Rope off Abandon the climb by abseiling down to the ground.
RPs Trade name for a popular type of micro-wire.
Rope-length A climbing distance equivalent to the full length of the rope.
Runner An anchor placed in the hope of minimising the length of a fall.
Run-out Distance climbed above the stance or last runner.
RURP Type of piton with an extremely small and slender blade (derived from the term Realised Ultimate Reality Piton).
Safety rope Secondary rope used to safeguard a climber when abseiling or prusiking.
Sandstone A fine-grained, compact, but sometimes unreliable rock type commonly found in Cheshire and south-east England.
Scoop A shallow depression in the rock face.
Scrambling Simple climbing on large holds.
Scree Unstable accumulations of stones found on or below cliffs.
Screwgate Alternative term for locking karabiner.
Second The climber who ascends the pitch second (as opposed to **leader**).
Serious climbing Climbing which is potentially dangerous, either because of loose rock or lack of protection.
Shoulder belay Early method of belaying, now virtually obsolete.

Side pull Vertically aligned handhold used to maintain balance.
Sit-harness Harness which supports waist and thighs and to which the climbing rope is attached.
Sit sling Improvised sit-harness.
Skyhook Metal hook placed over a tiny flake and used as an aid point for precarious support.
Slab Any expanse of rock angled approximately between 30 and 70 degrees.
Slings Loops of rope or tape having several applications.
SMC Scottish Mountaineering Club (major national club with responsibility for producing guidebooks).
Smearing Technique of using small, sloping footholds by applying the sole of the boot. Also refers to rock boots particularly suited to this technique.
Snaplink Alternative term for karabiner.
Soloing Unroped climbing.
Spike A finger of rock used as a hold or anchor.
Stance A ledge part-way up the route where climbers regroup.
Standard Alternative term for grade.
Star rating A means of indicating route quality in guidebooks by awarding a rating of one to three stars.
Static rope Low stretch rope used for accessory cord and other subsidiary purposes but not as the main climbing rope.
Sticht plate Alternative term for a belay brake.
Sticky boots Rock boots soled with high-friction rubber.
Stitched sling Webbing or tape commercially sewn into a loop.
Stomach traverse An ungainly crawl along a ledge on which it is impossible to

stand because of bulging rock above.
Stopper Trade name for popular type of wedge shaped nut. Also a general term for a particularly secure runner.
Strenuous climbing Climbing which drains strength and stamina.
Supertape Trade name for common type of strong webbing.
Sustained climbing Climbing of unrelenting difficulty.
Tape Nylon webbing.
Tape knot Knot used when making loops from nylon webbing.
Technical climbing Section of a route having several problematic moves.
Tension traverse Method of traversing using the rope tensioned through a nearby runner as partial support.
Terrace A flat area several metres wide and possibly extending the full width of the cliff.
Thin climbing Difficult climbing using small, infrequent holds.
Thread Anchor formed by feeding a sling through a natural rock tunnel or around a chockstone.
Through route Tunnel-like exit from a chimney.
Tie-off A short sling fixed around a partially inserted piton to reduce leverage.
Toe traverse A traverse furnished with footholds but, perversely, no handholds.
Topo Diagram showing the line taken by a route.
Top roping Method of safeguarding an ascent by first gaining the top of the climb (by means other than climbing) and throwing down a rope end.
Traverse Part of a route which involves climbing across instead of up.
Tyrolean traverse Spectacular but usually unnecessary method of crossing a ravine by sliding across a rope anchored to each side.
UIAA Union Internationale des Associations d'Alpinisme (international governing body of mountaineering).
UIAGM Union Internationale des Associations des Guides de Montagne (international union of qualified professional guides).
Undercut hold Upside-down hold used to maintain balance.
Undergraded Refers to a route on which the climbing proves more difficult than implied by the grade.
Unprotected Section of climbing where runners are poor or absent.
Vegetation Assorted plant life obscuring rock holds.
Vibram sole Trade name for a common type of treaded boot sole.
Waist belay Method of belaying without using a belay brake.
Waist belt A simple harness or the waist component of a sit-harness.
Wall Rock face angled steeper than about 70 degrees.
Wedge Method of climbing off width cracks using shoulder and leg jams. Also an alternative term for wedge-shaped nut.
Well protected Section of climbing where runners are reliable and frequent.
Wire Type of runner made from a nut threaded on a wire loop.
Yo-yoing Repeated attempts on a route where the leader is lowered down for a rest after each failure.

Useful Addresses

Association of British Mountain Guides
Private guiding and instruction. Contact through BMC.

British Mountaineering Council (BMC)
Crawford House
Precinct Centre
Booth Street East
Manchester M13 9RZ

Courses, publications, access, insurance, etc. This is the best single source of information and addresses.

Cordee Books
3a De Montfort Street
Leicester LE1 7HD

Main distributors of UK and foreign maps, guides, technical handbooks and narratives on mountaineering subjects.

Glenmore Lodge
National Outdoor Training Centre
Aviemore
Inverness-shire PH22 1QU

Mountaineering Council of Scotland
15 Dowiesmill Lane
Edinburgh EH4 6DW

Plas y Brenin
National Centre for Mountain Activities
Capel Curig
Betws y Coed
Gwynedd LL24 OET

Bibliography

GUIDEBOOKS

Listed here are club guides which give comprehensive information on some of the more popular British climbing areas (*see* Chapter 14 for fuller descriptions). These books are revised regularly and so titles may vary from year to year. Guides to less popular areas, and to climbs of mainly local interest, have not been included; these will be stocked as a matter of course by equipment suppliers in the areas concerned. Commercially published selected guides (not listed) are also available to most areas. These are most useful when first compiling a guidebook library and for first visits to an unfamiliar area. Most specialist retailers will stock the full selection.

The following abbreviations have been used for guide publishers:

SMC   Scottish Mountaineering Club
F&RCC   Fell & Rock Climbing Club
YMC   Yorkshire Mountaineering Club
BMC   British Mountaineering Council
CC   Climbers' Club

Scotland

Glencoe and Glen Etive (SMC)   Accessible climbing of all standards in Glencoe plus unique friction slabs in Glen Etive.
Lochaber and Badenoch (SMC)   Includes Ben Nevis; classic ridges plus hard routes on Carn Dearg.
Skye (SMC)   Medium grade classics on rough gabbro.
Cairngorms (SMC)   Wide variety of climbing, much of it on remote mountain faces.

Lake District

Langdale (F&RCC)   Good climbing on Gimmer and Pavey Ark among pleasant surroundings.
Scafell, Dow and Eskdale (F&RCC)   Long routes of all standards among the big fells.
Borrowdale (F&RCC)   Outcrop climbing in a delightful valley.

Northern England

Yorkshire Limestone (YMC)   Pleasant outcrops plus the forbidding walls of Malham, Gordale and Kilnsey.
Yorkshire Gritstone (YMC)   Uncompromising outcrop climbing at Almscliff and Brimham plus other venues for more private struggles.

Peak District

Stanage/Millstone (BMC)   Something for everyone on four miles of peerless Stanage grit. Powerful routes at Millstone Quarry.
Derwent Gritstone (BMC)   Several fine outcrops including the gentle slabs of Birchens and the brutal cracks of Curbar.
Staffordshire Area (BMC)   Gritstoner's Valhalla at the Roaches and Hen Cloud.
Peak District Limestone (BMC)   Mixture of peaceful riverbanks and thundering

road sides, but the climbing is the thing: steep, white and frightening.

North Wales

Ogwen (CC)   Classic routes in the lower grades for early climbs and first leads.
Llanberis Pass (CC)   Sombre valley with famous climbs in the middle and higher grades.
Clogwyn du'r Arddu (CC)   The best cliff in North Wales. Steeped in history.
Tremadog and Moelwyns (CC)   Sun-stroked outcrop climbing for experts at Tremadog; damper delights for beginners in the Moelwyns.
Gogarth (CC)   Sea, sun, and awe inspiring cliffs. Good climbs are HVS or harder.

Southern England and Wales

Pembroke (CC)   Miles of vertical sea cliffs and lots of sun. Endless one-pitch opportunities at HVS or harder.
Avon Gorge (Dark Peak)   Respectable (and respected) limestone walls near Bristol.
Southern Sandstone (CC)   Small outcrops gaining stature by virtue of their isolation.
West Penwith (CC)   Routes of all standards on Cornish granite; spiritual home of the sea cliff climber.

TECHNICAL BOOKS

The books listed here deal with peripheral aspects of the sport not covered in depth in the main text.

Ashton, Steve, *Hill Walking and Scrambling* (Crowood Press 1987). Describes the essentials of basic mountaineering in summer and winter.
Cliff, Peter, *Mountain Navigation* 2nd Edition (Peter Cliff/Cordee Books). Concise paperback to essential map and compass techniques.
March, Bill, *Modern Rope Techniques* 3rd Edition (Cicerone Press 1985). Intricacies of improvised rescue described in paperback with simple diagrams and concise text.
Pedgley, David, *Mountain Weather* (Cicerone Press 1979). Practical paperback guide.
Renouf, J. & Hulse, S., *First Aid for Hill Walkers and Climbers* (Cicerone Press 1982). Convenient paperback manual giving realistic advice on recognising and treating injuries.

GENERAL READING

Books listed under this heading reveal the tremendous scope for rock climbing in Europe, as well as giving additional insight into the world of the rock climber. Most are expensive hardbacks, but should be available to order from your local library.

Pause, W. & Winkler, J., *Extreme Alpine Rock* (Granada 1979). Armchair guide to 100 hard Alpine rock climbs with photographs, topos and historical background.
Rebuffat, Gaston, *The Mont Blanc Massif* (Kaye & Ward 1974). Superbly illustrated narrative/guide to the best on Chamonix granite. Guaranteed to convert rock climbers to mountaineering.
Wilson, Ken, (ed.) *Classic Rock* (Granada 1978). Well-illustrated sampler of the best

in Britain at Diff and Severe.

Wilson, Ken, (ed.) *Hard Rock* (Granada 1974). First and best loved of the illustrated British climbs series. Times have changed and these routes in the *VS* to *E3* category are now within every enthusiast's grasp.

Wilson, K. & Newman B., (ed.) *Extreme Rock* (Diadem 1987). State of the art British climbing in words and pictures.

MAGAZINES

Climber All aspects of British rock climbing and hill walking plus international mountaineering (monthly).

High Similar coverage to *Climber*. Official journal of the British Mountaineering Council (monthly).

Mountain International mountaineering and rock climbing (bi-monthly).

Index

Note: italic numerals denote page numbers of illustrations.

Abseiling 94–100, *95*, *99*, 103, *138*
    for new route inspection 106
    knot for joining ropes 59
    in the Alps 111, 112
    rope for 51
    using Italian friction hitch 58
    when soloing 115
Access restrictions 39, 134, 135
Accessory cord 54–5, 59
    for abseil cord 112
    for prusik loops 60
    for runners 66
    knots allowance 57
Aid climbing *107*, 107–110
    history of 118–19, 120
Alpine climbing 110–112
    history of 117, 118, 122
Arete climbing *71*
Artificial climbing (*see* Aid climbing)
Artificial climbing walls (*see* Climbing walls)
Ascenders (*see* Prusiking)
Avon 135, 151

Bandoleer 67, 110, 115
Belay anchors 80–82, *87–91*
    securing to 58, 60
    when abseiling 97–8, *99*
    when direct belaying *112*
    when soloing 114
Belay brake 45, *45*, 85–7, *87*
    carrying 68
    for abseiling *95–6*, 97
    karabiners for 55, *85*
Belaying 19, 80–87, 112–13

BMC 149
Bolts 109
Boots (*see* Footwear)
Borrowdale 128
Bouldering 9, 28–30, *30*, *32*, *41*, 70
Bowline 57, *57*
Bridging *72*, 76

Cairngorms 125
Camming devices 38, 62, 66, *66*, 68
Carreg Wastad 22–3
Chalk 29, 31, 38, 121
Cheating 40, 107, 122
Cheddar 135
Chimneys 27, 76
Chocks (*see* Nuts)
Climbing calls (*see* Communication)
Climbing walls 31–3, *33*
Clothing 38, 42–4, 48
Clove hitch 58, *58*, 81, *109*, 111
Communication 25, 80, *83–5*
Corner climbing 72
Cornwall *136*, 137, 151
Courses 14, 17, *17*
Cow's tail 109–110
Cracks 77

Dartmoor 137
Descenders (*see* Abseiling)
Devon 137
Diet 34
Dinas Cromlech 24–7, *37*, *121*, *138*
Direct belays 58, 112, *112*
Double fisherman's knot 59, *59*, 97
Double rope technique 98, *98*, 103

157

Index

Dow Crag 19, 26, 129, *130*

Equipment 38–9, 42–4, 46–9, 111–12
Escaping the belay 82, *102*, 103
Etriers 109–110
Extenders/extending runners 55, 63–4, *64–5*, 68, 91–3, *92–3*

Falls 16, 40
   arresting falls 86, *86*
   fall factor 88–9, *89*
   recovery/rescue 100, *102*, 102–105
   rope damage in 52
   when soloing 114–15
Figure-of-eight knot 58, *58*, 81, 112, 114
First aid 46–8, 103–104
First ascents 36, 94, 106–107, 117–22
Footwear 38, 42–3, *43*, 75, 111–12, 119, 121
Friends (*see* Camming devices)

Gower 12–14, 135
Glencoe *69*, 125
Grading 31, 35–6, 113, 119–22, 139–41
Gritstone 25, 75, *116*, *121*, 127, *129*, 130–33, *132*
Grooves 15–16
Guidebooks 10, 35–6, 139, 150–51

Harness 44–5, *44*
   attachment to 55, 57–8, *81*
   racking gear on 67–8
   when abseiling 95, *95*, 98
   when aid climbing 109–110
   when prusiking *101*
   when soloing *115*
Headtorch *47*, 48
Helmet 46, *47*
Hexentrics 61, *61*, *65*, 65–6, 68, *93*
History of climbing 10, 61–2, 107–108, 116–22

Improvised rescue 102–105

Indoor climbing walls (*see* Climbing walls)
Injury 33–4
International Distress Signal 104
Italian friction hitch 58, 58–9
   for abseiling 95–6, 97, 98
   for belaying 85–7, *87*, 102
   for direct belaying 112, *112*
   karabiner for 55

Jamming (*see* Cracks)

Karabiners 55–6, 67
   carrying 67–8
   for Italian friction hitch *45*, *59*, *96*, *112*
   locking *55*, *81*, *85*, 101, *115*
   ordinary *56*
   precautions with 92, *92–3*
   when abseiling 95–8, *96*
   when aid climbing 109–110
Klemheist knot (*see* Prusik loops)
Knots 57–60

Lake District 19, 24, 26, 117–20, *118*, *120*, 127–8, *128*, *130*, 150
Lancashire 30, 41, 127
Langdale 128
Laybacking 29–30, *73*
Limestone 75, *122*, 127, 130–31, *131*, 134–7
Llanberis Pass 22, 24, *134*
Loose rock 75, 106
Lowering 102–103
Lundy 137

Mantelshelves 74
Micro-wires 38, 56, 61, *65*, 65, 68
Mid-Wales 134–5
Milestone Buttress *16*
Moelwyns 134
Mountain rescue 104–105
Moving together 112–13, *113*

Index

New routes (*see* First ascents)
North Wales 11, 16, 18, 20, 23, 26, 37, 117–20, *119*, *121*, *133*, 133–4, *138*, 151
North York Moors 127
Northern Highlands 123
Northumberland 127
Nut key 46, *47*, 66, 68
Nuts 38, *61*, 61–2, *64*, *65*, 64–8, *92–3*, 108

Ogwen 133
Overhangs 78, *107*, 109, *121*
Peak District 25, *116*, 117–20, *121*, *122*, 130–33, *131*, *132*, 150
Pembrokeshire 135, 151
Pitons *108–109*, 108–110, 112
  as abseil anchors 94, 97
  tying off, 58, *109*
Protection 36
  equipment 38, 61–8
  retrieval 103
  when aid climbing 110
  when soloing 113–15
Prusik loops 46, 60, *60*
  carrying 68
  for abseil protection 98
  for escaping the belay *102*, 103
  for prusiking 100–101, *101*
  mechanical, for solo protection 114–15, *115*

Quarries *30*, *41*, 75, 127, 131

Rescue (*see* Mountain rescue)
Reversing 21, 22, 91, 103
Ridge climbing 24–5, 112–13, *113*
Rock boots (*see* Footwear)
Rope 50–54, *51*
  care of 52–4
  coiling *52–3*, 54, 112

  drag 25, 51, 55, *90*, 90–91
  technique 51, 80–93, 112–15
Rucksacks *48*, 49
Runners (*see* Protection)

Sandstone 75, 127, 137, 151
Scotland 69, 117, 123–5, *126*, 150
Sea cliffs 39, 94, 119, 123, 134–7
Sit-harness (*see* Harness)
Skye 125, *126*
Slabs 89
Slings (*see* Tape slings)
Snowdon 134
Solo climbing 13–14, 101, 113–15, *114*, 117
Standards (*see* Grading)
Stopper knot 57, *57*
Survival bag 48, 111

Tape slings 55, 62–3, *63*, 67
  allowance for knot 57
  knot for tape 59, *59*
  precautions with *92–3*, 103
  when abseiling 95, *95*
Top roping 17, 55, 91, *91*
Training 30–34, 36, 120
Traversing 26, 31, 87–8, *88*, *90*, 94
Tremadog *18*, *20*, *23*, 134, *135*
Tryfan 18–21

UIAA 46, 50–51, 139

Vegetation 75–9

Waist belay 85–6, *86*, 102
Wasdale 128
Wet rock 15–16, 39, 79

Yorkshire 127, *129*, 150

159